PENGUIN PASSNOTES

Hobson's Choice

Maureen Blakesley was born in Staffordshire and educated at the University of Keele. She is at present Head of the English Department at Longdean School, Hemel Hempstead, Hertfordshire.

PENGUIN PASSNOTES

HAROLD BRIGHOUSE
Hobson's Choice

MAUREEN BLAKESLEY, M.A.
ADVISORY EDITOR: STEPHEN COOTE, M.A., PH.D.

PENGUIN BOOKS

Penguin Books Ltd, Harmondsworth, Middlesex, England
Viking Penguin Inc., 40 West 23rd Street, New York, New York 10010, U.S.A.
Penguin Books Australia Ltd, Ringwood, Victoria, Australia
Penguin Books Canada Limited, 2801 John Street, Markham, Ontario, Canada L3R 1B4
Penguin Books (N.Z.) Ltd, 182–190 Wairau Road, Auckland 10, New Zealand

First published by Penguin Books 1987

Copyright © Maureen Blakesley, 1987
All rights reserved

Interactive approach developed by Susan Quillam

Made and printed in Great Britain by
Richard Clay Ltd, Bungay, Suffolk
Filmset in Monophoto Ehrhardt

Hobson's Choice was first published by Samuel French Ltd.

All rights whatsoever in the play are fully protected and application for permission to perform it by professional and amateur companies must be addressed to Samuel French Ltd, 52 Fitzroy Street, London, W1P 6JR. No performance may take place unless a licence has first been obtained.

Except in the United States of America, this book is sold subject
to the condition that it shall not, by way of trade or otherwise, be lent,
re-sold, hired out, or otherwise circulated without the
publisher's prior consent in any form of binding or cover other than
that in which it is published and without a similar condition
including this condition being imposed on the subsequent purchaser

Contents

To the Student	7
Background	9
Summary of the Plot	10
Commentary	21
Characters	45
Themes	58
Questions on *Hobson's Choice*	66
Glossary	71

To the Student

The purpose of this book is to help you to appreciate Harold Brighouse's play *Hobson's Choice*. It will help you to understand what happens during the play and why the characters speak and behave as they do. It will also help you to understand some of the themes which run through the work. When you have thought about these ideas a little more deeply, you will appreciate and understand the play much better and, more importantly, enjoy it much more.

You will need to read the play through several times and, if possible, see a performance of the play if it is being presented anywhere nearby. Unlike a novel, a play's whole purpose is to be acted on the stage before an audience, and if you can be a member of that audience then the experience is quite different from the one you have when you read the text. If you cannot see the play, you will have to use your imagination to see the characters on stage for yourself. Perhaps you could enact certain scenes with friends. Acting out a part is one of the best ways of understanding the playwright's intention.

You may be able to see the film which was made of the play. It is sometimes shown on television and may be available for hire. A combination of all these ways of seeing the play would help you to understand it and form your own opinions about it. Different interpretations will show that there is no absolute answer to the way it should be staged and that your opinion, provided you can always support it with evidence from the play, is just as important as anyone else's opinion.

This *Passnote* has been written to help you to form your own opinions by asking yourself questions about the play. Why does the playwright use particular themes for his play? Why do the characters behave in particular ways? Why is the play still performed today when it is concerned with the events of a century ago? You may be able to think of many other questions about the play, arising from your own interest in it.

When you know the play thoroughly and have worked through many of the questions – answering them in written form, in discussion or in dramatic work – you will be able to write persuasively and confidently about it.

Background

The writer of *Hobson's Choice*, Harold Brighouse, was born in 1882 and died in 1958. His childhood was spent in Eccles, near Manchester, and although he passed the scholarship exam to the Manchester Grammar School, he did not become a teacher, as his mother had been, but took a job learning to sell textiles.

He spent many of his evenings when he was a young man in the audience of Miss Horniman's repertory theatre in Manchester and when he was sent to work in London, he spent his time there watching plays. However, it was memories of his childhood near Manchester which inspired his most successful play, *Hobson's Choice*.

Together with two or three other playwrights, Harold Brighouse became known as a writer of the 'Manchester School' of dramatists. These writers used ordinary working people as characters in their plays, tried as far as possible to be realistic and, perhaps most important of all, used the everyday speech, the dialect, of the working people of Manchester. The attraction of *Hobson's Choice* to a Manchester audience came from all these points, as well as its great asset, that it was funny. An audience could laugh at the pomposity of Hobson and perhaps at the same time recognize the characters in the play as the kinds of people who were their neighbours and relatives.

Brighouse wrote many other plays, including several one-act plays which were very popular with amateur dramatic groups, and also half a dozen novels, but it is for *Hobson's Choice* that he is chiefly remembered.

If you would like to read more about Harold Brighouse, you can do so in his biography *What I Have Had* which was published in 1952.

Summary of the Plot

(*The page references are from the edition published by Heinemann Educational Books, 1964.*)

ACT ONE

Harold Brighouse's play *Hobson's Choice* has very detailed stage instructions: about the scenery, the appearance and age of the characters and the way in which the actors should behave and move. The play opens with a full description of Hobson's Boot Shop in Chapel Street, Salford. Any production of the play should be staged as closely as possible to the writer's intentions.

Whether we read the stage directions or sit in the audience when the curtain rises, revealing the set, we get the impression of a hard-working family who own a shop which keeps them in food and clothing, but is not luxurious or especially successful. Brighouse says 'There are no elaborate fittings', and describes the shop as 'dingy but business-like'.

We meet the three Hobson daughters: two are onstage when the curtains open and the entrance of the third, Maggie, signals the start of the play. Their immediate conversation is about their father, Henry Hobson, who is late getting up because he had been at a Masons' meeting the night before.

The first visitor is Albert Prosser, Alice's young man, who obviously expects her father to be out. They address each other formally as 'Miss Alice' and 'Mr Prosser', in the polite way that well-brought-up young people of the 1880s would do. Albert is keen to go when he discovers that Hobson is in, but he is immediately pounced on by Maggie, who not only keeps him in the shop but forces him to buy a new pair of boots. After the sale of the boots Albert is dismissed by Maggie with a brisk 'Good morning, Mr Prosser' as she holds the door open for him.

Alice is annoyed by this curt dismissal of her young man, pointing

Summary of the Plot: Act One

out that meeting in the shop is the only way to do any courting. Maggie is also curt, saying that courting is 'All glitter and no use to nobody'.

At this point Henry Hobson enters the play. He is dressed to go out and we soon learn from his daughters, although he tries to pretend otherwise, that he is going out for a drink at the local public house, 'The Moonraker's Inn'. Because Hobson has been found out, he decides to lecture his daughters, which he does in a pompous way, telling them that since their mother's death they have become 'bumptious', something he will not tolerate. He says that he is outraged by the fashionable clothes they have been wearing and especially by their bustles. His friends at the pub agree with him about how immodest this fashion is. Maggie is not included in this criticism, but when Alice and Vickey protest, Hobson widens his comments to include the virtues of the middle classes. He finally threatens to find Alice and Vickey husbands. At this point Maggie comes into the conversation once more, asking if she may not have a husband too. Hobson calls his words 'the brutal truth', and what he says does seem to the audience very unkind: 'if you want the brutal truth, you're past the marrying age. You're a proper old maid, Maggie, if ever there was one.'

Having given the girls his views and once again, or so he thinks, reasserted himself as the head of the family, Hobson prepares to go to the 'Moonraker's.' His departure is interrupted by the arrival of Mrs Hepworth, a wealthy, upper-class lady of the town. Hobson makes a fool of himself by kneeling and fondling her foot, only to be told by Mrs Hepworth, 'You look ridiculous on the floor'.

She has come for one purpose: to talk to the workman who made her boots, Willie Mossop, who appears onstage through a trapdoor, as if he has come upstairs from a cellar workroom. Hobson assumes that Mrs Hepworth has come to complain about bad workmanship, when in fact she has come to congratulate Willie and to tell him that he is to make all her boots in future. Mrs Hepworth cannot be persuaded by Maggie to order any more boots then and there, but she leaves her visiting card with Willie and promises to send her daughters to buy boots.

As she leaves, Hobson's drinking friend, Jim Heeler, arrives, clearly impressed by such high-born folks visiting Hobson's shop. Hobson sends the girls out of the shop so that he can have a serious discussion about his daughters and their ways, and especially about his hopes of getting them married off. When Hobson learns from Jim Heeler that he may have to pay settlements, or dowries, for his daughters, he changes his mind. 'I'd a fancy for a bit of peace, but there's luxuries a man can buy too dear. Settlements indeed!'

After Jim and her father have left to go to the public house, Maggie takes the opportunity to have a private word with Willie Mossop. She has decided that she and Will must marry and, because he is such a good bootmaker and she is so successful at selling boots, they will do well together. At first Willie does not understand what Maggie is proposing, but when she does make it clear, he has to sit down because he feels faint. Although he is flattered by Maggie's offer of marriage he tells her that he is not in love with her, and also that he is 'tokened', that is, engaged, to Ada Figgins. Maggie's response is direct: 'Then you'll get loose and quick'. Maggie tells Will that if he marries Ada, who is 'the helpless sort', he'll be 'an eighteen shilling a week bootmaker' for the rest of his life.

Ada Figgins brings in Willie's dinner and Maggie immediately tells her that she will have to give up her engagement with Will, saying that her own plans for Will's future are better than Ada's. Ada comments weakly, 'It's daylight robbery'. When she realizes that she has lost Will, she threatens him with the anger of her mother who has organized the engagement. However, when Willie realizes that he need not go back to his lodgings with Ada and her mother, he is very relieved. 'It's like an 'appy dream. Eh, Maggie, you do manage things.' Maggie tells Will to arrange for the banns to be read so that they can be married in three weeks.

Alice and Vickey enter the shop again from the house and Maggie gives them the news of the forthcoming marriage. The two sisters are shocked and Alice shows her snobbery when she says, 'Look here, Maggie, what you do touches us, and you're mistaken if you think I'll own Willie Mossop for my brother-in-law.' Almost immediately Henry Hobson returns from the Moonraker's, with only one thought in his head – his dinner. The girls try to tell him about the proposed marriage between Maggie and Will and when Hobson understands, his first thought is that such a decision should have been his. 'Didn't you hear me say I'd do the choosing when it came to a question of husbands?' But he is still more concerned about his dinner!

When Maggie confronts him, Hobson tries to give reasons for disliking the marriage, saying 'Why, lass, his father was a workhouse brat'. He is also concerned with his own image in the town if Maggie marries one of his workmen. 'I'd be the laughing-stock of the place if I allowed it.' When Maggie continues to argue, pointing out how much hard work she has done all her life, telling Hobson what he should pay her now, his reaction is to call Will up immediately and try to beat him with a leather belt. This infuriates Will and we see the first sign of independence in him when he defies Hobson and kisses Maggie. 'And if Mr Hobson raises up that strap again, I'll do more. I'll walk straight out of shop with thee and us two 'ull set up for ourselves.'

Maggie is proud of him and so ends the first act of the play. Hobson 'stands in amazed indecision'.

ACT TWO

This takes place one month later and is again set in Hobson's shop. Now that Maggie has left, her two sisters, Alice and Vickey, are in charge of the shop. We soon learn that all is not well: the girls have no idea what orders to give Tubby, the foreman bootmaker, about what stock to make. Trade has been slack and Hobson has become difficult and bad-tempered since Maggie left. The girls are low in spirits because they think that they have no chance of getting married now. Vickey says, 'Maggie's spoilt our chances for ever. Nobody's fretting to get Willie Mossop for a brother-in-law.'

We meet Freddy Beenstock, Vickey's young man, when he comes into the shop in the company of Maggie and Will. Maggie is in an organizing mood and sends Freddy to fetch Albert Prosser, who has not been in the shop to see Alice since Maggie and Will announced that they intended to get married.

Maggie wants to take advantage of the fact that her father has had too much to drink at the public house, has walked along the street and has fallen through an open trapdoor in the pavement, into Beenstock's cellar warehouse. He is still there, sleeping off his drunkenness on some bags of corn.

While Freddy is away, Alice and Vickey take the opportunity to be unkind to Will by hinting that it is because of his forthcoming marriage to Maggie that their own prospects of getting married have fallen so low. Maggie insists that they accept him as a member of the family and also insists that both her sisters give Will a kiss as a token of friendship.

When Alice asks Maggie why she and Will are at the shop on a work day, Maggie explains that there are two reasons. The first is that she has a plan which will help to bring about the marriages of her two sisters, the second is that it is Maggie and Will's wedding-day. The girls are invited to the church for the wedding ceremony in the afternoon and to their cellar home in the evening for a wedding-celebration.

Vickey and Alice are scandalized when Maggie picks out a brass ring for her wedding, and even more so when they learn that Maggie and Will mean to start married life with secondhand furniture. Maggie and Will have brought a hand-cart round to Hobson's so they can take away any unwanted bits of furniture from the lumber-room upstairs. When the girls see the broken chairs, they almost claim them for themselves, but Maggie insists that the furniture be put on the hand-cart so that Will can repair it in the afternoon and it will be ready to use that evening.

When Freddy and Albert come into the shop, Maggie immediately organizes them into carrying the furniture downstairs. Maggie has already hinted to her sisters that she has a plan which will get 'marriage portions' for them; she will tell them about it after the wedding. She questions Albert about the legal document which he has been drafting. Albert is not sure that it is absolutely sound in law, but he reads out

Summary of the Plot: **Act Three**   15

the document, which is an action against Henry Hobson for trespassing on the property of Beenstock, corn merchants. You will remember that it is in Beenstock's cellar that Hobson is sleeping off his drunkenness.

Freddy and Albert have loaded the hand-cart by now and Maggie once again organizes everyone. Freddy is to go to Beenstock's cellar and pin the legal document on Hobson as he sleeps; her two sisters are to get ready to be at the church on time for the wedding and Albert is to take the hand-cart of furniture through the streets to Maggie and Will's new home. Tubby is called up from the cellar and told that he is to be in charge of the shop while everyone is out.

With all the rest of the characters off-stage, Maggie takes the opportunity to have a quiet word with Will about whether he wants to go through with this wedding ceremony. Will replies that he is resigned, that she is growing on him and he will go through with it. Vickey and Alice reappear dressed in their Sunday clothes and all four set off for the church – with Maggie looking after the ring!

ACT THREE

This act takes place in the cellar in Oldfield Road which is Will's and Maggie's home. They are now married and Alice and Albert, Vickey and Fred have come home with them to celebrate their wedding. They have had a meal of pork pie. There is a small wedding-cake and there is tea to drink. When the curtain rises the four visitors are drinking cups of tea to toast the health of the bride and groom.

Willie has obviously learnt by heart a short speech – part of which he forgets – thanking his visitors for coming to the wedding and for wishing him and Maggie well. Albert is keen to make a speech himself and begins to do so, rather pompously, only to be told by Alice to sit down immediately.

Freddy Beenstock congratulates Will on his speech; Albert is interested in where they borrowed the money to start their own business. Maggie tells him mysteriously that it was from the same place as the hot-house flowers which are decorating the table. All of them realize that it will not be long before Henry Hobson wakes up from his drunken sleep in Beenstock's cellar and discovers the lawyer's note pinned to his coat.

Meanwhile, the three young men are persuaded by Maggie into doing the washing-up, although with some protest from Freddy and Albert. While Maggie and her sisters are off-stage for a few minutes, Will confides to Albert and Fred how nervous he is to be left alone with Maggie, even though they are married. Just as they finish washing up, a knock is heard at the door. They know it is Henry Hobson and Vickey, Alice, Freddy and Albert are all scared of his temper. They agree to go into the bedroom, leaving Maggie to deal with her father. Hobson ignores the notice which Maggie had hung on the door, saying 'Business suspended for the day' and comes in. Maggie tells him that she will have to ask her husband for permission for him to come down into the living-room.

Will soundly shakes his new father-in-law by the hand and Maggie invites him to take a cup of tea with them and most especially, to eat a piece of their wedding-cake. This would be a blessing on their marriage. Hobson is reluctant, but Maggie insists.

He has, of course, come to talk about the letter which he found when he woke up from his drunken sleep. Maggie insists that he should discuss it with Will, but Hobson wants to talk about it with Maggie. Eventually he agrees that Will shall hear what the matter is.

He sees the letter – an action for damages for trespass – as bringing ruin on him, especially because he thinks of himself as such an upright, respectable man. But even when Maggie asks him whether it was an accident, Hobson will not take the blame for being drunk and falling through the trapdoor, but instead blames Maggie, saying that because of her ingratitude he has had to drink his sorrows away. He is frightened that the publicity will lose him customers from his shop, especially since he would have to confess in court that he was drunk at midday.

He is not soothed by the thought that the story might even be reported in *The Guardian* and that he could hardly continue to be church-warden after that! Hobson is comforted, however, by Maggie's suggestion that perhaps this action of trespass might be settled out of court and then there would be no publicity at all. At this, Albert and the others come back onstage. Hobson's first reaction is to be aggressive because his daughters are not looking after the shop; then he threatens them, saying that because of their defiance, their wedding-days will be a long way off.

Albert suggests that £1000 would be enough to prevent the case from coming to court, but this is too much for Hobson. Even Maggie thinks it is unreasonable. They settle on £500, and Hobson gives his word that he will pay that amount. When Maggie announces that this will be divided between the two couples so that they can afford to get married, Hobson thinks he has been cheated. He becomes more and more angry and finally leaves the room shouting abuse at them all.

The two young couples wish everyone goodnight and quickly go; leaving Maggie and Will together. Will fetches his slate, sits at the table and prepares for another writing lesson from Maggie. As an exercise, she sets him to copying the sentence 'Great things grow from small'. Meanwhile Maggie throws out the hot-house flowers which were a present from Mrs Hepworth, keeping one to press in her Bible as a memento of their wedding-day.

Maggie goes off to bed, leaving Will writing his lesson on the slate. He is too shy to go into the bedroom, and after several false starts eventually settles down to sleep on the sofa. The bedroom door opens and Maggie, in her night-dress, leads Will through the bedroom door by his ear!

ACT FOUR

This act takes place a year later and is set in Henry Hobson's living-room which, since his daughters have left home, is very untidy and dirty. Tubby Wadlow is cooking bacon over the fire for Hobson's breakfast and as he does this Hobson's drinking friend, Jim Heeler, arrives. Apparently Hobson has asked Tubby to run and fetch Dr MacFarlane and Jim Heeler because he believes he is very ill.

While they are waiting for Hobson they discuss trade and Tubby reveals how slack things are. Maggie had a way of selling shoes and clogs which men do not have, and Will is such a good bootmaker that customers go to him now rather than to Hobson's.

When Hobson does arrive he is very sorry for himself. He thinks he should have his daughters with him now that he feels so ill and he even refuses Tubby's bacon. He tells Jim that he has sent for the doctor because he is dying. He is so depressed that the only use he can see for water is to drown himself; he has not washed, and has had to throw his razor away in case he cuts his throat with it! It is drink, he confesses, which has been his downfall.

Dr MacFarlane, 'a domineering Scotsman of fifty', now enters, and is annoyed to find his patient out of bed. He has been sent for early in the morning after he has been up all night delivering a 'first' baby. Both Hobson and Jim look alike to him – both are men who drink too much and he mistakes one for the other. It is Hobson's turn to be annoyed when the doctor sees immediately what Hobson's problem is. Jim does not help matters by interrupting the doctor when he is trying to talk to Hobson. In fact, Jim has to leave.

After examining Hobson, the doctor diagnoses his illness as chronic alcoholism and prescribes both medicine and giving up drink completely. Even after Hobson has heard the doctor's opinion, that he has drunk himself within six months of dying, he still will not agree: he refuses to take any medicine and he refuses absolutely to give up alcohol. The two men are evenly matched in determination, so much so that Dr MacFarlane is absolutely determined not to let this patient die.

He questions Hobson about his wife, and whether he has any other female relative who would look after him. Hobson's wife is in heaven, he says, and his three daughters are all 'queerly married'. It is Maggie who has become most 'uppish' says Hobson and when Dr MacFarlane hears that, he declares that Maggie must be the one to cure Hobson. Just as the two men are discussing Maggie, in she comes! In fact,

Summary of the Plot: Act Four

Tubby Wadlow has gone out and called on all three of the sisters, telling them to come and see their father, who is very ill.

Maggie is not keen to come back to look after her father but is finally persuaded by Dr MacFarlane that Hobson will drink himself to death unless he is properly looked after. After the doctor has left, Maggie asks Tubby to fetch her husband, Will, and also to go to the chemist to get the prescription made up.

Hobson is scornful of Maggie's needing to ask Will's permission, believing that Will is still the weak man he remembers from a year ago. In the middle of this discussion, Alice enters, rather more elaborately dressed than a year ago and rather proud now. She is quite rude to Maggie, pointing out that a woman of her class would not rise as early in the morning as a working woman like Maggie. Alice feels that she cannot be expected to come back home to look after her father after the sort of home she has become used to since her marriage. Instead, she expects Maggie to give up her home.

At this moment, Vickey comes onstage and immediately makes a tremendous fuss of her father. However, she cools a little when she learns that her father expects her to come and live with him, to look after him. Her excuse is that she is pregnant and that her expected child is more important to her than her father. Maggie thinks very little of this excuse; any one of them could become pregnant, she says. Meanwhile she has persuaded her father to put a collar on and smarten up a little before Will comes. Hobson is astounded by this but agrees to do so on the grounds that his neck is cold!

The three girls squabble about who should come back home to look after Hobson, with Maggie insisting that she needs to ask Will before she can make any decision. Her two sisters are quite scornful of this, knowing that their own husbands would have to agree to whatever decisions they made! While Maggie is out in the shop talking to Will, Vickey and Alice realize that if Maggie does come back home, Hobson might leave the business to Maggie and Will, with no money at all to his other two daughters. Alice thinks it would be wise if Albert Prosser drew up Hobson's will before this could happen.

Vickey discovers Will next door in the shop inspecting the stock, and when he comes onstage he is much more self-confident than a year ago. He judges the business to be worth only £200 now, and scandalizes Vickey by suggesting that her husband should know because he is in trade too.

The two sisters soon discover that they cannot order Will around as they used to and that he and Maggie will come back to look after Hobson only on their own terms. When Hobson comes in, Will is anxious to settle the terms so that he can go back to his own shop and not lose business that day. The two girls stay, they say, to make sure that their father is not cheated by Will, but in fact they have their own interests at heart. Hobson resents their attitude and, after again asking Vickey and Alice whether they will come and look after him, he tells them to leave. They are quite angry, and do so, although Maggie and Will are pleasant to them as they leave.

Now comes the time for bargaining! Hobson still has not realized that Will is an independent young businessman who will not come back to his old job and his old pay. Will explains in no uncertain terms how their business has been thriving in the last year and how he has taken all the trade away from Hobson's shop.

He is prepared to move in with Hobson, take a half-share in the business – as long as Hobson does not interfere – and call the shop 'William Mossop, late Hobson'. Even Maggie thinks this is going rather far and when Will insists, they eventually agree upon 'Mossop and Hobson'. Will talks about the alterations he will make and the way in which the new, improved business will bring in high-class trade. He is ambitious now. Hobson goes out to find his hat so that he can walk along to Albert Prosser's to sign the deed of partnership. No other course of action is open to him – it is 'Hobson's Choice'.

In his absence, Maggie and Will agree that Will's confidence carried them through; Maggie is proud of him. When he tries to replace her brass wedding-ring with a gold one, however, she disagrees. The brass one has been good enough for her, she says, and will remain so. When they are rich it will remind them of their poor and humble beginnings.

The play ends with an affectionate touch. Maggie says 'Eh, lad!' and touches Will lovingly. Will responds with 'Eh, lass!' and kisses her. Hobson has put his hat on and is now ready to go out. Willie can hardly believe his good luck; he is the master now!

Commentary

ACT ONE

When the play opens, the audience can see a realistic stage-set representing an efficient but rather ordinary boot and shoe shop in Salford in the 1880s. Imagine that you knew nothing at all about the play, what sort of play would you expect from such scenery?

Two of the actresses are on stage when the play begins and one more enters immediately – the three Hobson girls. The audience can tell from their clothes that they are not wealthy. They wear black, with neat black aprons, say the stage directions, so they are obviously workers of some kind. We soon learn their situation – three daughters running a boot and shoe shop with a father who drinks – but it is all very matter-of-fact; they are not sorry for themselves. Try to put yourself in their position. What would it be like working for your own father, probably with no wages except your clothes and food? Write a paragraph in which you imagine you are Vickey or Maggie confiding to a close friend what you really feel about the situation at home.

After a minute or two Albert Prosser comes onstage. He is Alice's young man and is obviously using Hobson's absence to have a word with Alice. When he learns that Hobson is not out, he tries to leave. Why, do you think, does he do this? Is he really frightened of Hobson or merely embarrassed that he might be caught flirting with Alice in working hours? If you were Alice's father, what attitude might you have towards Albert? Would you be pleased or annoyed that such a well-dressed lawyer is courting your daughter?

It is Maggie who captures Albert's attention. She obviously thinks very little of young men who come to flirt with her sisters and she realizes she can turn this to advantage. Since it is a shop, it is a reasonable assumption that Albert has come to buy something. He, of course, when asked what he wants to buy, thinks of the cheapest thing — a pair of bootlaces. Is this quick thinking on his part, do you think, or has he prepared an alibi beforehand, in case he should be caught? What would you have said in Albert's position?

In fact Maggie ignores this request and sets about fitting him with a new pair of boots. She does not ask him whether he wants them, she just fits them on him. The stage directions tell us that Albert 'simpers', that is, smiles in a foolish way, but he soon stops when he notes that Maggie is not smiling. She organizes the boots, insists that Albert walks about in them to make sure they fit and then boxes up his old boots to be mended and sent home with the bill for the new ones. Albert is completely defeated. In fact he says, 'Well, if anyone had told me I was coming in here to spend a pound I'd have called him crazy.'

What do you think of the way Maggie behaves? Is she too forthright or do you think she was entitled to behave in this way? Do you like her or dislike her, admire her or despise her? Why? Give your reasons.

Imagine you are Albert Prosser, having bought a pair of boots you didn't want or need. How do you feel about it? Do you think it will make you feel more kindly towards the Hobson family? Will it encourage you to visit Alice more or to stay away from the shop?

The third person who is involved in this transaction is Alice. Albert is, after all, her young man and he has just been humiliated before her eyes by her bossy sister, Maggie. She says 'Maggie, we know you're a pushing sales-woman, but —'. She is obviously annoyed by the way Maggie has treated Albert and retaliates by being spiteful: 'It's all very well for an old maid like you to talk'.

Do you think Alice should have interfered? Should she have protected her young man from Maggie's salesmanship? What would you have done if you had been Alice?

Now that Albert has left the stage, what impression did you get of his character? Write a short paragraph giving your opinion of him, using the evidence of what he says and does as the backbone of your argument.

Commentary: **Act One** 23

The new person to enter is the man of the title of the play, Henry Hobson himself. The author, Harold Brighouse, has delayed Hobson's entrance until about ten minutes into the play, although the audience has already heard a great deal about him. We have learnt that he has been out the night before at a Masons' meeting and may have a hangover; we know that it is his custom to go out for a drink at The Moonraker's Arms; and we know that Albert Prosser comes to see Alice when he believes her father to be out. All of this builds up a picture in our minds of what Hobson might be like. Why do you think the playwright organizes the play so that we have to wait to meet Hobson? Why isn't Hobson onstage when the curtain goes up?

The playwright also gives detailed stage instructions about Hobson's appearance, 'successful, coarse, florid, and a parent of the period'. He wears a heavy gold chain with masonic emblems on it, which tells us that he is obviously very proud to be a Mason.

His announcement that he is 'just going out for a quarter of an hour' is treated with scorn by his daughters, who know very well that he is going to the public house and will probably be more than an hour. From the way all three daughters join in, it is clear to the audience that this is a frequent occurrence. In fact, it seems that they go too far in testing his authority because he decides to lecture them on their behaviour.

What is your view of this conversation? Do you think Hobson's daughters are justified in speaking to him in the way they do or do you think they are rather cheeky to their father? Would you have reacted in the same way as Hobson does or would you have ignored them and gone out to the 'Moonraker's'?

Hobson takes a chair and straddles it in an aggressive way rather than sitting on it properly. Why do you think he does this? He doesn't speak to them as much as lecture them and continues in spite of Maggie's remark, 'I expect Mr Heeler's waiting for you in "Moonraker's", father.' Hobson takes the view that his daughters are 'rebellious' and that 'There's been a gradual increase of uppishness towards me'. He is extremely forthright in his choice of words, telling his daughters that they are not only uppish but also bumptious and that he hates bumptiousness like he hates a lawyer – which may well explain why Albert Prosser felt he was so unwelcome when Hobson was at home.

Do you agree with Hobson? From what you have seen do you think his daughters are uppish and bumptious? Why do you think Hobson refuses to answer Maggie's question 'How much a week do you give us?' Do you think he gives them anything? Do they deserve anything?

The next conversation is concerned with clothes and the fact that Vickey and Alice have just had new dresses. Although £10 a year seems very little to us now, it was quite a reasonable sum then to spend at the tailor's. Of course the audience will laugh because it sounds a ridiculously low amount. What Hobson particularly objects to is the 'hump added to nature', the bustle, at the back of the girls' dresses. What is more, Hobson is outraged because the publican at the 'Moonraker's' – 'As honest a man as God Almighty ever set behind a bar, my ladies' – also disapproved of the hump. He thinks the fashion is 'immodest'.

This argument seems a timeless one because parents always seem to object to their children's clothes, whether they have bustles or wear miniskirts, tight jeans or punk clothes. Do you think that such a conflict about clothes and appearance is inevitable? Do your parents like the way you dress and have your hair? How will you behave when you are parents yourselves and your own children wear clothes which you don't like?

Hobson is in full flow now about the dreadful behaviour of his daughters and takes the opportunity of telling them what kind of man he is, and how they are disgracing him. 'I'm a decent-minded man. I'm Hobson. I'm British middle class and proud of it. I stand for common-sense and sincerity.' His solution to all this uppishness and bumptiousness on the part of his daughters is not to conquer it but to pass it on to other people – their husbands. 'I'll choose a pair of husbands for you, my girls. That's what I'll do.' Hobson obviously regards his daughters as his property, to do with as he chooses. It is true that girls of the 1880s had very little independence and were often financially dependent on their fathers and husbands.

It is now the turn of Maggie to be outraged by Hobson's criticisms, because she has not been included in the plan for husbands. The

Commentary: Act One 25

stage directions tell us that Hobson is astonished at her belief that she too should have a husband and he laughs at her. In fact, Hobson is quite unkind to Maggie, saying, 'But if you want the brutal truth, you're past the marrying age. You're a proper old maid, Maggie, if ever there was one.'

Maggie says very little to this except, simply, 'I'm thirty'. How do you think she feels about being spoken to in this way? Do you think she has a plan in mind? How would you have reacted if you had been Maggie?

Having apparently settled this problem, and brought his daughters to order, Hobson prepares to leave home to go to the public house but he stays a little longer because he sees an important customer, Mrs Hepworth, getting out of her carriage outside the shop. He rather overdoes the politeness and flattery, making himself look foolish in the eyes of Mrs Hepworth. She is very forthright; 'Get up Hobson. You look ridiculous on the floor.'

She has come to the shop to discover who has made her boots and because Hobson thinks she has come to complain about them, he is very evasive. She turns to Maggie in exasperation and Maggie calls Tubby Wadlow up into the shop. From Tubby Mrs Hepworth learns that the bootmaker she wants to see is called Willie Mossop. When Will appears we see a poorly dressed workman, very quiet and humble.

If you were Willie working down in the cellar making boots, what would you expect to be in store for you if Tubby called you up into the shop to meet a rich lady? When the lady says 'Take that', Willie expects a blow on the head but discovers that 'that' is a visiting card with Mrs Hepworth's address on it. Willie cannot read it. He confesses that he can only read 'a bit' and not at all when the printing is in italics, as it is on the card. Would you expect Willie to be embarrassed by his inability to read or do you think he just accepts it?

Hobson misunderstands all that is going on and still thinks that Mrs Hepworth is complaining. He apologizes, saying, 'I assure you it shall not occur again, Mrs Hepworth.' He is astonished when he finally realizes that she is praising Will's handiwork and then annoyed when Mrs Hepworth says, 'The man's a treasure, and I expect you underpay him.' Hobson quickly dismisses Will and when Mrs Hepworth has gone, grumbles about her. 'I wish some people would mind their own business. What does she want to praise a workman to his face for?'

Do you think Will has understood all this? He is in the cellar workroom now, clutching Mrs Hepworth's visiting card and perhaps trying again to read the spidery print.

Hobson shows his hypocrisy. When Mrs Hepworth was in the shop, he was embarrassing with his fawning flattery but as soon as she has left he says, 'Last time she puts her foot in my shop', and, 'Thinks she owns the earth because she lives at Hope Hall.'

Next we meet a new character, Jim Heeler, Hobson's drinking partner at the 'Moonraker's'. He was surprised to see a carriage with Mrs Hepworth inside it outside Hobson's shop. Hobson again lies, 'Why, I've made boots for her and all her circle for ... how long, Maggie? Oh, I dunno.'

Hobson is still worrying about his daughters and decides to send his daughters away so that he can tell all his troubles to Jim Heeler. The two men discuss how they cope with their daughters and Hobson confesses that he misses his wife's part in bringing them up. In spite of being grateful for the quiet since his wife died, 'the dominion of one woman is Paradise to the dominion of three'.

Jim flatters Hobson by likening Hobson's ability to talk with that of John Bright, the great orator. Even Hobson sees through this. 'Nay, that's putting it a bit too strong. A good case needs no flattery', although he may be fishing for even more flattery – which is what he gets!

From their conversation Hobson and Jim Heeler obviously agree about women; it is easy to see why these two men are friends. Jim, without prompting, comes to the same conclusion as Hobson had done earlier. 'Then you quit roaring at 'em and get 'em wed.' He thinks it will be easy enough to find husbands for them as long as Hobson is not looking for 'angels in breeches'. The bad news which Jim breaks to Hobson is that paying for weddings will not be all he has to do; he may have to find dowries for his daughters, or, as he calls them, 'settlements'. This is a shock for Hobson. 'I've changed

Commentary: **Act One** 27

my mind. I'd a fancy for a bit of peace, but there's luxuries a man can buy too dear. Settlements indeed!' When Jim points out that at least Hobson would save their wages, we learn what we have already suspected. 'Wages? Do you think I pay wages to my own daughters? I'm not a fool.'

The talk of paying out money is too much for Hobson and he decides that now the 'Moonraker's' is the right place to be. Both men leave, but only after another altercation with Maggie about what time dinner is to be.

Now that the audience has met Jim Heeler, what is your impression of him? List all the reasons you can think of which make the two men friends. Why do you think the playwright allowed the audience to hear this conversation about Hobson's daughters and marriage rather than letting the two men talk it out in the public house? Why didn't the scene shift to the 'Moonraker's'?

After her father and Jim have gone, Maggie stays onstage and calls Willie Mossop up through the trapdoor. The stage instruction says he comes 'reluctantly' and when asked to show Maggie his hands, he does so 'hesitatingly'. Why, do you think, is Willie reluctant and hesitant?

Like Mrs Hepworth, Maggie too praises Willie. 'You're a natural born genius at making boots.' He does not understand what Maggie is getting at and even thinks that he may lose his job. Even when Maggie points out that it is his workmanship and her salesmanship that keep the shop going, telling him 'We're a pair, Will Mossop', he still does not follow her train of thought, or if he does he will not admit it. When it does occur to him, he backs away. 'I'll be getting back to my stool, Miss Maggie.' In fact he is so overcome that he needs to sit down. He still fears that she is proposing marriage to him and when she proposes a 'working partnership' he is very relieved indeed. 'Partnership! Oh, that's a different thing. I thought you were axing me to wed you.' Her reply of, 'I am,' astounds him even more. 'And you the master's daughter.'

Will is very honest in his reaction to this sudden proposal, saying that 'It's a bit awkward-like' and eventually blurting out, 'I'm bound to tell you that I'm none in love with you.' Maggie thinks that this is no barrier, since she loves him, but Will is still very worried about Hobson's reaction. His further objection to their being married is that he is already engaged – to a girl called Ada Figgins. Maggie deals with that stumbling-block in her quick, characteristic way. 'Then you'll get loose and quick. Who's Ada Figgins?' In Maggie's eyes Ada is a 'scheming hussy', because she has had the same idea about Will as Maggie has.

Will has no ambition and is not at all keen on Maggie's idea of marrying him, saying, 'I wish you'd leave me alone.' The situation is further complicated by the entrance of Ada Figgins with Will's dinner in a basin. Ada reveals that Will is a bit of a musician and that she's in love with him. She is not pleased when Maggie reveals her plan to marry Will, insisting 'You'll pardon me. You've spoke too late. Will and me's tokened.'

The scene on the stage is quite funny now with two girls quarrelling over a man – the reverse of the usual situation. Will is both funny and pathetic, relying on Ada to save him from Maggie's clutches. 'Aren't you going to put up a better fight for me than that, Ada? You're fair giving me to her.'

When Maggie discovers that Ada's mother is involved in organizing the engagement between Will and Ada – Will confesses, 'She had above a bit to do with it' – she decides that Will must not go back to his lodgings with the Figgins family again but can stay with Tubby. Will's relief at this news overwhelms him. 'It's like an 'appy dream. Eh, Maggie, you do manage things.'

Maggie, having decided on a course of action, is keen to get on with things and orders Will to go to the vicar to put up the banns. The banns announcing the marriage have to be read in the parish church on three consecutive Sundays before a couple can be married. Not only must Will do this but Maggie says he must also kiss her, which Will thinks is 'forcing things a bit'. However, Will is saved from this embarrassment by the entry of Maggie's two sisters.

So now the marriage is arranged between Maggie and Will. Everything happened very quickly. What were your feelings during this scene? Were you sorry or pleased for Will? What is your opinion of the way Will behaved when the two girls were arguing about which

Commentary: Act One 29

one he should marry? Should he have stood up for himself a little more?

And what of Maggie? Do you think she was justified in taking Will away from Ada? They were engaged, after all. Is she being purely selfish, thinking only of her own future? Do you believe Maggie when she says she loves Will? Do you think a marriage built on only one partner loving the other will succeed or fail?

Now comes another difficult situation for Will because Maggie breaks the news to her sisters that she and Will are to be married. Their snobbery is revealed immediately; Alice thinks that this will affect her chances of marrying Albert Prosser. Hobson comes home and after some chat in which he tries again to show that he is head of the house and will not be ordered about, he too is shocked to hear the news about Maggie and Will. Like Alice he thinks of himself first. 'Didn't you hear me say I'd do the choosing when it came to a question of husbands?' His snobbery too is illustrated when he says, 'You can't have Willie Mossop. Why, lass, his father was a workhouse brat. A come-by-chance.' He is not concerned with Maggie's future happiness but only with his image in the neighbourhood. 'I'd be the laughing-stock of the place if I allowed it.'

When Maggie sets out the financial proposals for Hobson paying Will's wages and wages now to Maggie, who has never been paid, Hobson's anger gets the better of him. He responds violently; he takes off his leather belt in order to beat Willie but in return Will kisses Maggie and threatens that both of them will walk out of the shop forever! Maggie is overjoyed at Will's strength of character, saying 'Willie! I knew you had it in you, lad.' She puts her arm round his neck; he is astounded and Hobson is too.

When the curtains close at the end of Act I we have met several people and a great deal has happened. This is a fast-moving play and in the theatre we have to concentrate to hear every reply and reaction. There might well be an interval now.

What have you enjoyed most in Act I? Which of the characters have you liked most and least? Give your reasons.

If you did not know the story, how would you expect it to go on now? Is everything settled or will there be continuing conflict in the

Hobson household? What will happen to Alice and Vickey? Do the events you have just seen make you want to see the rest of the play or do you think the end is inevitable? How many different ways can you think of developing the plot?

ACT TWO

The scene is a month later, still in the Hobson shop. The audience knows that it will take three weeks for the banns to be read in church so now it is time for the next stage in the plot – Will and Maggie's marriage.

It soon becomes clear that Vickey and Alice are trying to run the shop in Maggie's absence but that things are not going too well. They are not sure what orders to give Tubby about making boots or clogs and their arithmetic is too weak to cope with the finances of the shop. Hobson still spends his time drinking, leaving his two daughters to run the shop.

The girls are still being snobbish in their attitude towards Will. 'Nobody's fretting to get Willie Mossop for a brother-in-law.'

Maggie and Will come on stage at the same time as another character whom the audience has not yet met. He is Freddy Beenstock, Vickey's young man, and it soon becomes clear that he has told Maggie of his wish to marry Vickey and of Hobson's opposition to the idea. Maggie clearly has an idea which will break this deadlock and she sends Freddy to fetch Albert so that all of them can organize themselves together. Before Freddy goes, he reveals that Hobson, coming home drunk, has fallen into a cellar through a trapdoor in the pavement and is now snoring away in the Beenstock corn warehouse.

After he has gone, Maggie discusses with her sisters their chances of getting married, only to find them still sulky and rude about having Will in the family. They insult Will to his face but Maggie points out that, after all, her sisters are only shop assistants and Will is his own master. What is more, she then orders her sisters to kiss

Commentary: Act Two

Will since he is to be their brother-in-law. After a little hesitation they do so!

Do you think it is fair of Maggie to insist that her sisters kiss Will? Will it make them like him more or less? He quite enjoys the kisses, saying, 'There's more in kissing nice young women than I thought.'

Do you think Vickey and Alice were justified in being ashamed of Will? What effect do you think their snobbery would have on him?

Maggie reveals that their reason for being in the shop today is that it is their wedding-day and the girls are invited to the wedding. They can leave the shop to Tubby, especially as trade is not very brisk. Once more they are ashamed of Maggie when she chooses a brass ring to be married with, and even more so when she announces that she and Will have bought some secondhand furniture to set up house. But they change their views a little when Maggie sends Will up to the lumber-room, to look at the broken furniture again, wondering if it would do for them when they are married.

The plan to get the girls their 'marriage portions' is still in Maggie's mind but she refuses to reveal the details before they go to the church. Maggie organizes Freddy and Albert when they arrive, Freddy to help carry a sofa downstairs and Albert to write a legal document which is an action against Hobson for trespass on the premises of Beenstock, Corn Merchants.

It is getting late, and it is almost time for the wedding. Freddy is sent to pin the legal document on Hobson's coat as he sleeps and Albert is told that he must take the old sofa through the streets on a hand-cart to Maggie and Will's new home. He is not pleased and hopes that none of his friends will see him, but he realizes that there is no alternative if he wants Maggie to continue with the plan which will help him to marry Alice. Tubby is left in charge of the shop.

Before the wedding Maggie asks Will if he can be honest in the marriage vows he is about to make and Will's reply is 'Yes, Maggie. I'm resigned. You're growing on me, lass. I'll toe the line with you.'

Off they go to the wedding, with the girls in their Sunday clothes, Maggie in charge of the brass wedding-ring and Tubby throwing old shoes after them to wish them luck.

Act II, like Act I, is fast-moving and eventful. A lot happens.

32 *Passnotes:* Hobson's Choice

Perhaps the most important thing is Maggie's plan to bring their father round to their way of thinking, to agree to Vickey and Alice being married — even to distributing marriage settlements. The plan is a kind of blackmail because, as Albert has admitted, his 'legal' document would not hold up in a court of law.

How do you see the plot going now? Compare what has happened in Act II with the notes which you made at the end of Act I. Would you have altered it?

What impression do you get of Will now? Has he changed at all? Write down five words which you think would describe him now. Expand the list into a paragraph of description.

ACT TWO

The set has changed to the cellar living-room which is going to be home for Maggie and Will. Will's name is seen on the windows and the room is furnished very sparsely. Will has now mended the furniture from Hobson's lumber-room. They are drinking a health in tea to the bride and bridegroom and have obviously been celebrating the wedding with pork pie and wedding-cake.

When the curtain rises, Will is on his feet making a speech which he has obviously tried to learn and in which he has to be prompted by Maggie. Albert's attempted response, however, is cut short by Alice who says, 'We've had enough of speeches.' Will's speech has surprised the others and he confesses that he has been learning a lot lately. Maggie is educating him.

Albert is intrigued about where Maggie and Will found the money to start their own bootmaking business. Alice had wondered the same thing in Act II. Can you find Alice's question and discover how Maggie answered it? Why, do you think, was Maggie so vague? This time Maggie tells them that the money came from the same place as the flowers. Albert understands. Do you understand? Who do you think is rich enough to have lent Maggie and Will the money for their business? Why is Maggie so mysterious?

They begin to be worried about Hobson waking up in the Beenstock

Commentary: Act Three

corn cellar and discovering the note pinned to his jacket and they realize that it is time the girls went home. Before they all go, however, Maggie organizes them into clearing the table so that Will can use it for his writing lesson later. Albert and Freddy are outraged to discover that they are expected to help with the washing-up. In a conversation with Will they discover that he is not as keen as Maggie that everyone should rush away because he is rather nervous of being left alone with Maggie. Albert and Freddy do nothing to help his nervousness, saying it was he who married Maggie and he must cope on his own. They are interrupted by Maggie who has come to see how they are getting on with the washing up.

A knock on the door precedes Hobson's entrance into the room. All of them except Maggie are worried about how he will act, so she ushers them into the bedroom offstage and prepares to deal with her father herself. Will is told to stay because he is the 'gaffer', the head of the household.

The first part of Maggie's plan is that her father should acknowledge that Will is master and that she needs to ask his permission for her father to stay. Hobson has to make it up with Will by shaking his hand although Will again sees a way of escaping being alone with Maggie by saying, 'I hope you'll see your way to staying a good long while.' Maggie encourages her father to drink a cup of tea, eat a piece of pork pie and also a slice of wedding-cake – obviously something he has always hated.

Hobson is very subdued, which is why he gives in to Maggie so easily. He obviously has a headache after drinking so much and is very worried about the legal document he has found. He desperately needs to talk to Maggie about it but she will not hear of such a thing, insisting that he should talk to Willie. She even insists that Will calls Hobson 'father', something which neither Hobson nor Will is very sure about. Eventually he agrees – he has no choice – that he will discuss his problem with both Maggie and Will.

Do you think this is fair of Maggie? If you were Hobson and were in disgrace, would you want Will to know about it? Or do you feel that Hobson has brought all his misfortunes on himself and so has to behave as Maggie instructs him?

Hobson reveals his belief that he is ruined and starts one of his ranting speeches about his own importance, only to be interrupted by Maggie. Hobson sees the action for trespass as 'a stab in the back; it's an unfair, un-English, cowardly way of taking a mean advantage of a casual accident.' He tries to blame the whole thing on Maggie saying that he stayed too long at the 'Moonraker's' in order to drown his sorrows at the thought of his 'thankless child'.

Maggie, in the middle of Hobson's flood of self pity, asks twice if it was an accident, and eventually Hobson admits that it was an accident but once again indulges in a torrent of words, this time about lawyers. Maggie does not comfort her father; in fact she adds fuel to the fire by saying, 'I shouldn't wonder if you didn't lose some trade from this.'

Hobson is afraid of this and especially of losing his reputation in the neighbourhood by having to admit in court to being 'overcome' at twelve o'clock in the morning; he cannot bring himself to admit that he was drunk.

Both Maggie and Will encourage Hobson to believe that his escapade will be reported in the local paper and Hobson even believes it might get into the *Manchester Guardian*. The playwright's stage direction tells us that Willie 'is perfectly simple and has no malicious intention', but we know that Maggie is clever enough to realize that the more frightened Hobson is of his disgrace becoming public knowledge, the more likely he is to fall in with her plans. In fact, because Will is so naïve, he does not realize how upset Hobson is becoming, especially at the thought of losing so many customers from the church where he is a warden. Hobson is angry and starts calling Will names.

Maggie calms him by suggesting that perhaps there need be no publicity if Hobson is prepared to settle the case out of court, and then astounds him by opening the door and calling Albert Prosser. After Hobson has discovered, and is disgusted by, the fact that Albert is a lawyer, all the rest of those who had been in the bedroom reveal themselves. Hobson's first thought is of who is looking after the shop, then he is outraged that Maggie has given orders for Tubby to look after it.

Hobson is obviously not completely cowed by his ordeal and by the prospect of dealing with lawyers and he is capable of some anger when he thinks his daughters have flouted his orders. Do you think he is justified in being angry at this point?

Even Maggie's explanation that they have left the shop because it is her wedding-day does not placate Hobson; he retorts that, 'It'll be many a year before there's another wedding in this family.'

Albert's intervention, suggesting they get down to business, serves to inflame Hobson even more, especially as he has said so often how much he hates lawyers. He is astonished by Albert's demand for £1000 to settle out of court and even Maggie is inclined to think 'That one thousand's too much'. She knows that Hobson can afford £500, and Hobson is grateful to her for pointing out that the negligence was not entirely on his side because the Beenstocks left the cellar flap open.

Hobson is still not persuaded that he should pay £500, but when Maggie again mentions the publicity and Vickey points out that he has not been beaten because the sum has been reduced by half, he agrees, although not very enthusiastically. However, when he learns that the £500 is to be used to finance his two daughters' marriages, his anger boils over and picking up his hat, he storms out, telling them what he thinks of them all as he goes and warning the young men how difficult life will be when they are married.

After Hobson's exit, it is the turn of the other four visitors to say goodnight, although Will is quite keen that they should stay. Alice has the grace to thank Maggie for organizing her sisters' weddings. Now it is time for Will's lesson and on the slate he has written 'There is always room at the top'. His new lesson is 'Great things grow from small'.

Why do you think Maggie gives Will sentences such as these to copy rather than, say, poetry or excerpts from the Bible?

Maggie shows a gentle side to her nature when she keeps one of her wedding flowers as a keepsake in her Bible. She also reveals to the audience, if they have not already guessed, that it was Mrs Hepworth who sent the flowers – the same person who financed their business.

The act ends without words. Will takes off his shoes and then his collar but cannot pluck up enough courage to go into the bedroom.

Eventually he settles down to sleep on the sofa only to find that Maggie comes back onstage, 'takes him by the ear, and returns with him to bedroom'.

Will this raise a laugh in the audience? If so, why? Would you have ended Act III in the same way as Brighouse does? If not, give your ending and explain your reasons.

A great deal has happened in Act III. Make a quick checklist for yourself of all the things that have happened; against some of them write what could come of them in the future. What do you think will happen in Act IV?

Have your opinions about any of the characters changed? Write a paragraph about Maggie and another about Will showing what new things you have learnt about them in Act III.

ACT FOUR

In this act the scene changes to Hobson's living-room which is next to the shop which we saw in Acts I and II. The room is overcrowded and dirty and the action takes place a year after Act III. The curtain rises to reveal Tubby Wadlow cooking breakfast over the fire and trying to lay the table at the same time.

Almost immediately Jim Heeler arrives, having been sent for by Hobson who says he is very ill. Dr MacFarlane has been summoned too, although Hobson is not so ill that he cannot get out of bed.

Knowing Hobson's character as you do, what kind of illness do you think he is suffering from? Why should he send for his friend as well as sending for the doctor?

While they are waiting for Hobson to appear, Tubby and Jim discuss the fortunes of the shop and the fact that trade has dwindled to almost nothing, although Jim does feel that perhaps Tubby should not discuss Hobson's private affairs. Tubby, however, is keen to talk and is quite sure that the Hobson business is failing not only because there is a rival bootmaking firm run by Willie and Maggie but also because there are no young ladies in the shop now to fit customers'

Commentary: Act Four

boots and shoes. Tubby also feels that much of their downfall is due to Hobson's lack of tact!

When Hobson enters, the stage direction tells us that he does so 'with acute melancholy and self-pity'. This self-pity is soon illustrated by Hobson saying, 'I'm deserted by them all and I'll die deserted, then perhaps they'll be sorry for the way they've treated me.' He believes he is dying, even though before this he has never been ill in his life. He hasn't washed and has not shaved in case he cuts his throat with the razor.

At least Hobson faces the truth when Jim asks the reason for his illness. He admits it is drink.

Their discussion of the effects of alcohol is interrupted by the entry of Dr MacFarlane. The stage direction describes him as 'domineering'. The doctor is not pleased to be called out so early, especially to a patient who is 'up' after he himself has been awake all night attending a childbirth.

The doctor can soon detect the 'fate' written on their faces. What does he mean by this? Hobson is rather put out by the plain, blunt speaking of this Scottish doctor who tells him that his 'complaint and ... character are the same'. What do you understand by this remark? How does Hobson's character influence his complaint?

Jim Heeler, too, is soon put in his place by the doctor who tells him to keep his mouth shut. Hobson realizes that Jim should go, but before he does, tells him that the only reason he is allowing the doctor to stay is in order to teach him a lesson. He is quite rude to Dr MacFarlane about how much he is paying for advice but the doctor does not seem to be insulted.

What impression do you have of the doctor so far? Do you think this is the first time he has come across anyone like Hobson? How does he deal with him?

Hobson knows that it is alcohol which has made him so ill and yet is infuriated by the doctor's suggestion that he should give it up. He makes it sound less dangerous by calling it 'reasonable refreshment'. In fact he is so infuriated by the doctor telling him the truth that he becomes even more stubborn than before, saying that he is ready to go down to the 'Moonraker's' immediately. It is this stubbornness that makes Dr MacFarlane try again, calling Hobson a 'pig-headed animal'.

The contest between them heats up, Dr MacFarlane having become by now exceedingly angry. His anger brings out his Scottish accent more strongly than before and he shouts down any objections from Hobson. He knows that Hobson needs someone to take a strong hand with him, to stop him drinking and to look after him. He discovers that the most 'uppish' of Hobson's daughters is Maggie and it is Maggie whom he prescribes to cure Hobson. Hobson is totally against this suggestion but the doctor is adamant, saying 'I've taken a fancy to ye and I decline to let ye kill yeself.'

Just as he is talking about Maggie, in she walks. Tubby Wadlow has obviously gone to tell her about her father's illness. The doctor insists on telling her the truth about her father's condition, even though Hobson is embarrassed by it. She needs to know all the details before she makes the decision to sacrifice her own home. Hobson is contemptuous of this idea; 'Sacrifice! If you saw her home you'd find another word than that. Two cellars in Oldfield Road.'

The doctor leaves, not with his tail between his legs as Hobson thinks, but in the belief that this has been a good morning's work and that Hobson's life is saved. He leaves three prescriptions — a written one for medicine and two others: total abstinence and being looked after by Maggie.

But the future is not yet clear. Maggie insists that she cannot make the decision to leave the business in Oldfield Road and come and look after her father without her husband's consent. Hobson is very scathing of such an idea, saying 'You know as well as I do asking Will's a matter of form.'

Is Hobson right, do you think? Is Maggie merely being polite in saying that she needs to ask Will's permission or would his views really influence her own?

Hobson clearly believes that he should have first call on Maggie's time and attention and also that it is clearly her duty as the eldest daughter to give up her own home and come back to him. In the middle of this conversation, Alice enters. The playwright tells us in

Commentary: Act Four

his note that 'She is rather elaborately dressed for so early in the day, and languidly haughty.'

Her first remarks show that she is still as snobbish as ever, comparing Maggie with herself, now 'a fashionable solicitor's wife', living in the Crescent. She insists that she could not possibly come back home to look after Hobson because it would lower her standard of living. However, before this conversation becomes too heated, in comes Vickey.

Vickey is as emotional and effusive as ever and gushes over her father thinking that he is ill. Hobson is equally sentimental, calling her 'My baby!' and declaring, 'At last I find a daughter who cares for me.' However, as soon as she learns that one of his daughters is needed to look after Hobson, her attitude changes somewhat, especially since she cannot in her 'circumstances'. Vickey whispers to Maggie to explain her 'circumstances'.

Why do you think that she cannot say outright that she is pregnant? Why does she need to whisper?

Maggie does not respond in any way to this news but changes the subject by asking her father to put his collar on before Will comes. Both Hobson and Vickey jump in quickly with remarks that show that they still regard Will as lower than they are in social status. Alice's snobbery is of a different kind, insisting that her father would put a collar on 'in any case'. Hobson agrees to do so, but in order to save his own pride he says 'it's not for the sake of Will Mossop. It's because my neck is cold.'

While Hobson goes to put on a shirt-collar, the three girls take the opportunity to discuss which of them is going to come back home to look after him. Alice has already declared that she has grown too used to living in the Crescent to give it up now, and Vickey, in spite of all her show of love and concern for Hobson when she first came, now insists that, 'My child comes first with me.' Alice believes it is Maggie's 'duty' to come back home and Vickey thinks it is more than a duty – it is a 'pleasure'. Neither of them can see any alternative.

Maggie, however, will not be so easily persuaded. She feels that she has already done more than her duty by living with Hobson for thirty years. She insists that she must talk to Will about it. Vickey is extremely insulting about this idea, saying that 'Will Mossop hasn't the spirit of a louse and we know it as well as you do.'

If you were Maggie how would you react to a remark such as this? She takes the insult very calmly, merely saying 'Maybe Will's come on since you saw him, Vickey.' Is this the best way of dealing with an insult, do you think? Think of a time when someone was rude to you or rude about someone you cared for. What did you say and do? Was that the best way of dealing with it or did you regret it later?

Before the subject of their conversation, Will, is called onstage from the shop, where he has been checking the stock, and while Maggie is temporarily out of the way, asking Will to come in, the two other sisters take the opportunity of discussing whether it is wise to let Maggie move back. Although they will not take responsibility for Hobson themselves, they are wary of letting Maggie do so in case she makes any money out of it. They are afraid that in his will Hobson will leave his money to Maggie and Will Mossop. This can be avoided if Albert Prosser draws up the will at once.

They are also reluctant to leave Maggie too long in the shop with Will. As Vickey says, 'She's only telling him what to say, and then she'll pretend he thought of it himself.'

When Will enters he has changed from the last time we saw him, in Act III. The stage direction tells us that 'He is not aggressive, but he is prosperous and has self-confidence.'

How has this come about, do you think? Make a list of the things you have already heard about which have happened in the past year and which might have given Will self-confidence.

Practically the first thing that happens when Will comes onstage is that he orders Maggie about! He tells her to fetch her father downstairs because time is short. He surprises the girls by his remark that Hobson's *was* a good business in its day – a remark which annoys both Alice and Vickey. They obviously prefer to think that it is much more prosperous than it actually is. Perhaps the talk about Hobson's will and what he is to leave to them is still in their minds.

Not only does Will annoy them by downgrading the value of their father's business in their opinion, but he follows this by suggesting that Vickey's husband, Fred Beenstock, is 'in trade'. Vickey is very

Commentary: Act Four

insulted and tries to distinguish between 'wholesale' trade which is the Beenstock business and retail trade like a boot-and-shoe shop.

Vickey still speaks to Will as if he is the humble employee he once was, asserting that 'the value of father's shop is no affair of yours, Will Mossop'. He thinks it is but Alice too tries to put Will in his place by saying 'You'll do what's arranged for you', and 'Will Mossop, do you know who you're talking to?' The squabbling goes on with Vickey spitefully saying 'Some folks get on too fast'.

Will makes a telling point when he mentions the fact that the sisters too got on in the world, but only because Maggie and Will arranged their marriage portions.

Whose side are you on in this argument? Is it one-sided or are there good arguments on both sides?

Hobson and Maggie come in. Will is very polite to Hobson to begin with but then says 'There used to be room for improvement'. Will wants to hurry along the negotiations about Hobson's shop because his own shop is being left unattended in the meantime, and he is losing trade. He makes it clear to Hobson that he worries about him only because Maggie is worried and that his business is more important to him than Hobson's state of health. He is extremely forthright in his attitude towards Hobson, even to the extent of being checked by Maggie. Will almost gives himself away by saying 'You told me to take a high hand, didn't you?'

When Alice and Vickey interfere, Hobson and Will temporarily team up against them, Will wanting them to stop interfering and Hobson wanting them to go because neither of them would give up her home to look after him. Their idea of protecting him against Will infuriates Hobson even further and pushes him into the sort of speech we heard from him in the first act, saying, 'I've fight enough left in me for a dozen such as him.'

Hobson insists on hearing both Alice and Vickey deny that they are willing to come back to look after him, confident that Maggie will do so. He practically orders them out, saying, 'I understand you've homes to go to.'

What is really in Hobson's mind, do you think? How does he imagine the future with Maggie looking after him?

Vickey and Alice are very insulted at being ordered out, although Maggie is polite enough to invite them to tea on Sundays 'sometimes'. Vickey leaves with what she imagines to be a witty criticism of those she leaves behind. 'Beggars on horseback' means that she is accusing them of pretending to be grander and more important than they really are. Such a remark is ironic coming from Vickey because it describes her perfectly well!

Hobson has been waiting for the girls to go so that he can put his proposals to Maggie and Will about the terms on which they may come back to live with him. He thinks he is being generous when he offers Will his old job and old wage back again with Maggie both keeping house and looking after the shop. He thinks 'if that's not handsome, I dunno what is. I'm finding you a house rent free and paying half the keep of your wife'.

Hobson seems to have forgotten very quickly how recently he had been so ill that he needed to see the doctor and that Maggie had had to be persuaded to stay. His arguments with his daughters seem to have excited him so much that he seems well again, well enough to set out terms for Maggie's return which are obviously unacceptable.

Do you think Hobson honestly believes that Maggie and Will will return on these terms or is he starting off with an extreme offer, hoping to compromise later? Remember, he has been 'in trade' all his life and is used to bargaining.

Will's and Maggie's reaction is immediate. They rise to go because Hobson's offer seems so ridiculous to them. Whether this reaction is prearranged we do not know but certainly both of them agree that Will's business is more important than listening to unacceptable offers. The stage direction here says that Hobson is 'incredulous', meaning 'unbelieving'. He honestly cannot see that Maggie and Will could turn down such a good offer.

It is now time for Will to put the record straight, making his longest speech in the play. He tells Hobson in plain terms that he and Maggie have worked hard and have thrived; they have paid back Mrs Hepworth's loan; they have taken away all Hobson's high-class trade and now Hobson offers them jobs which are the same as they were before they were married.

Commentary: Act Four

Hobson is obviously still living in the past or at least refusing to recognize that circumstances have changed. He still sees Will as 'my old shoe hand'. Hobson's interruptions only serve to fuel the fire of Will's passion. He puts forward his proposal to close his own business and to move back to Hobson – to merge or even to take over Hobson's business – with Hobson as a sleeping partner with no rights to interfere. Hobson is almost speechless at this suggestion.

Will's proposal to name the new business 'William Mossop, late Hobson' brings protests from Maggie and a few minutes are spent arguing over the new name, as if Hobson has already agreed to Will's proposal.

The audience will find this quite funny. Again there are three people on stage, as there were when Maggie wrenched Will away from Ada Figgins and one of them is helpless while the other two argue. Last time it was Will, this time it is Hobson who is outwitted. Both times Maggie is the winner of the argument! They settle on 'Mossop and Hobson'.

After the decision over the name, the next step is the practical alterations, with Will casting a critical eye over the state of Hobson's shop. He proposes more expensive chairs for the customers and carpet on the floor. Hobson is horrified at such extravagance.

Willie is in his element now. With everything settled he can see the prospects in Hobson's business, even forecasting that they will be in Saint Ann's Square in Manchester next. The last thing to be settled is the legal document setting out the deed of partnership and Will suggests that Maggie should take her father for 'a bit of fresh air' to Albert Prosser's lawyer's office. Hobson obediently says, 'I'll go and get my hat'. There is nothing else he can do – it is 'Hobson's Choice'.

In his absence Maggie and Will discuss what has happened and Will is almost sorry that Hobson is so defeated. 'He's crushed-like, Maggie. I'm afraid I bore on him too hard.' Will has been astounded by his own strength, saying, 'You told me to be strong and use the power that's come to me through you.' Maggie agrees with this, saying, 'You're the man I've made you and I'm proud.'

The play ends with Will trying to persuade Maggie to wear a gold wedding-ring now that they can afford one but Maggie agrees only if she can keep the brass ring as well to remind them, when they get 'too rich and proud', where they began. The scene ends in affection with Maggie saying, 'Eh, lad!' and Will kissing her, saying, 'Eh, lass!' Hobson appears with his hat on ready to go to the lawyer's and Will's last words are 'Well, by gum!'

Does this ending complete the story for us? Is it a story of 'they lived happily ever after' or not? Should there perhaps be another act continuing the story? If you think so perhaps you could outline the rest of the plot.

Do you regard this play as having a happy ending or a sad ending? Explain your reasons.

Are you satisfied with the end of the play? Does it tie up all the 'loose ends' for you or is there something you are not sure about?

Were you surprised at the end of the play or did you think it was inevitable?

Characters

HENRY HOBSON

The playwright describes Hobson in the stage directions as 'fifty-five, successful, coarse, florid, and a parent of the period'. He has a high opinion of himself and it is not until the very end of the play, when he meekly agrees to a partnership with Will, that his spirit is broken.

As soon as he comes on stage Hobson establishes himself as a pompous man. He *addresses* his daughters rather than talks to them and we feel that they have every reason for wanting to marry and leave home if this is the way they are treated. His style of speech is very blunt and to the point: 'I'm talking now, and you're listening', and he proclaims to the audience what kind of man he is. He obviously has a very clear image of himself when he says 'I'm a decent-minded man. I'm Hobson. I'm British middle class and proud of it. I stand for common-sense and sincerity.'

In fact it soon becomes clear that he has very little common-sense or he would have realized that it is Maggie's salesmanship and Will's bootmaking skills which make the shop prosperous while he, Hobson, is drinking at the local public house. It cannot be sound commonsense to treat them so badly when they clearly have the option of leaving him and setting up in business themselves.

His claim of sincerity is also untrue. He tries to give the impression that he is going out on important business when his daughters know quite well that he is going out to drink with his cronies at the pub. Nor is he sincere in his behaviour towards Mrs Hepworth. She can easily tell that he is flattering her to the point of embarrassment, fondling her foot.

His daughters leave him to marry and it is clear to the audience that Hobson is not able to look after himself. All his bluster and important talk cannot hide the fact that both his health and his business are deteriorating. He drinks so much that he cannot trust himself to shave in case he cuts his throat. When he encounters Dr MacFarlane he has met his match for stubbornness, because the doctor, like Maggie, is not fooled by Hobson's brave words. He prescribes Maggie as the cure for Hobson's complaint. It is a case of two strong-minded people trying to save Hobson.

Finally Hobson's spirit is broken when he agrees to Will being his partner and the new name of the shop being 'Mossop and Hobson'. The stage direction tells the actor playing Hobson to look 'pathetically' and rise from his chair 'obediently'. However, at the end of the play the audience suspects that in the future, life with Hobson will still not be plain sailing. He has for too long been the master in his own house to change overnight.

Find five quotations from the play which you think best illustrate the personality of Henry Hobson. Do *you* think he changes by the end of the play or do you think he is only temporarily crushed? How would you have reacted to the doctor's diagnosis if you had been Hobson?

Write a paragraph for someone who has not yet seen the play, describing the kind of man Hobson is.

MAGGIE HOBSON

Although the title of the play is concerned with Henry Hobson, Maggie is in fact the most important person in the play. It is she who organizes the lives of practically everyone else and without her the Hobson family would have gone on as before, gradually losing money and becoming failures. She organizes her sisters' marriages, her own marriage to Willie, and finally, the link between the two shoemaking businesses.

Ask yourself why she is so good at organizing other people and why she does it. Albert Prosser can see the danger of letting Maggie

Characters: Maggie Hobson

get her own way when he says 'If we start giving in to her now, she'll be a nuisance to us all our lives' (Act III page 42).

She is extremely useful to her father, running the business while he is out drinking at 'The Moonraker's'. Hobson compares his three daughters when he is talking to Jim Heeler, saying 'Vickey and Alice are mostly window dressing in shop. But Maggie's too useful to part with. And she's a bit on the ripe side for marrying, is our Maggie.' Why is he so sure, do you think, that Maggie will remain a spinster?

When Maggie proposes marriage to Will it is obviously something she has planned beforehand. She is quite practical in her view of marriage but it is clear by the end of the play that the marriage is based on affection. It is Maggie's strength of purpose which changes Will from a weakling to a man firm enough to organize the partnership between himself and Hobson, although it is clear that he has been coached by Maggie.

In spite of her practical ways, Maggie shows some softness of character. She does not really need to organize the marriages of her two sisters yet she does so; although she throws away the beautiful flowers sent by Mrs Hepworth on her wedding-day, she keeps one of them pressed as a memento; and finally in spite of the business-like reason she had for marrying Will, it is clear that she is very fond of him. At the end of the play the stage direction says, 'She touches him affectionately', and then Will kisses her.

Perhaps Maggie may seem rather formidable to the audience and yet it cannot be that she is completely hard. Although she comes back to look after her father in return for Will's partnership, Hobson will not be an easy man to live with. She feels a sense of duty which her sisters do not, although their refusal to look after their father is, in part, snobbery.

Do you think Maggie changes during the play or is her character basically the same throughout? Find some examples to support whichever view you take.

How do you think Alice and Vickey regard Maggie at the beginning of the play? Are they frightened of her, scornful of her, or what? Has their opinion of her changed by the end of the play?

WILLIE MOSSOP

Willie has a low opinion of himself at the beginning of the play but by the end is speaking up for himself and is quite proud. It is the influence of Maggie which has made this change come about. He is proud at the end because he is successful.

Think about the effect that a success has had in your own life. How do you feel if you have done well or have been praised? How does being praised affect the way you think about yourself? Now imagine how Willie must have felt.

At the beginning of the play Willie emerges from the cellar – a trapdoor on the stage – and is humble. Brighouse describes him as 'a lanky fellow, about thirty, not naturally stupid but stunted mentally by a brutalized childhood'. He also says Willie has 'potentialities', which means the 'possibilities of doing well'. It is Maggie who has seen this possibility in Willie and it is she who exploits it for the good of all of them. His greatest potentiality is that he is an excellent bootmaker. Maggie says, 'You're a natural born genius at making boots. It's a pity you're a natural fool at all else'. (Act I page 15)

This remark is only half true, however, because although Willie continues to be an excellent bootmaker, he soon shows that he is not a natural fool. He stands up for himself when Maggie insists that they should marry; 'when it comes to marrying, I'm bound to tell you that I'm none in love with you.' (Act I page 17) However, this independence of spirit seems to disappear when the two girls, Maggie and Ada Figgins, squabble over who should marry him, and he pleads, 'Aren't you going to put up a better fight for me than that, Ada? You're fair giving me to her.'

What effect do you think a remark like this would have on the audience watching the play? Would they find Willie amusing, pathetic, tragic or what?

The reaction of the Hobson family towards Willie gradually changes throughout the play. Henry Hobson thinks of him as 'A decent lad. I've nowt against him that I know of' (Act I page 22), although he still thinks of him as the son of a 'workhouse brat' (Act I page 23). When Willie tries to give Hobson some advice about the action for damages for trespass, Hobson's pride still stands in the way of accepting help from his humble former employee: 'I didn't come to you, you jumped-up cock-a-hooping –' (Act III page 50). However, in spite of everything, Hobson has to admit to Willie that, 'Take you for all in all, you're the best of the bunch. You're a backward lad, but you know your trade and it's an honest one' (Act III page 55). At the end of the play Hobson has to agree to the new name of the shop, with Willie's name first.

Maggie's two sisters show that they are snobs when they learn that Willie is to be one of the family and can hardly believe the news. Alice immediately protests with 'you're mistaken if you think I'll own Willie Mossop for my brother-in-law' (Act I page 21).

Faced with such snobbery and with Henry Hobson's disapproval, Willie shows that he is a stronger character than we thought at first. He confronts Hobson at the end of Act I, kisses Maggie and threatens to leave. Willie and Maggie's wedding-night, however, shows Will still afraid of Maggie and an object of fun in the eyes of Albert and Freddy. It is his marriage to Maggie and the way she treats him which gradually give him confidence, until at the end of the play he is able to be masterful and successful.

Write down five words or phrases which you think describe Willie at the beginning of the play and then another five words or phrases which describe him at the end.

How would you feel if a person like Willie married one of your relatives? Would you feel proud or ashamed? Give your reasons.

ALICE HOBSON

Alice is the middle daughter in the Hobson family; she comes between Maggie, the oldest and bossiest, and Vickey, the youngest and prettiest. She, like Vickey, is completely self-centred, caring only for what is best for herself. She is a snob, seeing marriage to Albert Prosser as a step up the social ladder, away from the 'trade' of Hobson's bootmaking business.

She is moderately independent, although no match for Maggie, who sees through the meetings of Alice and Albert and takes the opportunity to sell Albert a pair of boots which he did not need. Alice stands up to her father a little more, especially over the matter of the fashionable clothes which she and Vickey like to wear. 'It's not immodest, father. It's the fashion to wear bustles,' she tells him. However, she is not independent enough to know how to run the shop and organize the stock after Maggie has left.

Marriage is an escape from the shop and she is wise enough to see that Albert Prosser's ambition to be a prosperous lawyer fits well with her own. With her newly acquired status she scorns the working-class husband of Maggie, declaring, 'you're mistaken if you think I'll own Willie Mossop for my brother-in-law', and, 'Ah, well, a fashionable solicitor's wife doesn't rise so early as the wife of a working cobbler.' The stage directions tell us that after her marriage she overdresses and becomes 'languidly haughty'. She still, in Act IV, thinks she can order Willie around: 'You'll do what's arranged for you,' but is easily defeated when Will and Maggie point out the realities of the situation.

Like Vickey, she is not prepared to sacrifice her new life to come back home to look after her father, in spite of her suspicions about what might happen to the business after Hobson's death.

Imagine you are Alice. Describe a typical day in your life *before* the play opens. Then describe another day *after* the play is over. Are you happier?

How do you think Alice's life would have developed if Maggie had not interfered and helped Alice and Albert to marry?

Write down five words or phrases of your own which you think sum up Alice's personality for you.

VICKEY HOBSON

Vickey is the youngest of the three Hobson daughters and the prettiest. Her father tells her, 'You're pretty, but you're bumptious', but

Characters: Vickey Hobson

she knows that the truth is that he is proud of her looks. 'You like to see me in nice clothes,' she tells Hobson, and when he criticizes the fact that his daughters have been wearing new dresses, Vickey asserts, 'We shall dress as we like, father, and you can save your breath.' She is scandalized to think that her father has been discussing the bustles she wears on the back of her dresses with his drinking friends.

Although it is the money from Hobson's shop which pays for her pretty dresses, she is not concerned with running the business efficiently, preferring to sit and read. After Maggie marries, neither of the girls have much idea about what orders to give Tubby about the stock, and her marriage to Freddy Beenstock seems to be a suitable escape for her from the trade world of Hobson's boot business.

She seems to be a self-centred girl, caring little about others, even when the responsibility is partly her own. She snaps at Alice, 'That's your look-out' about ordering the stock and clearly has a reputation for lying when her father says, 'Vickey, you're pretty, but you can lie like a gas-meter.'

Although she seems outwardly affectionate towards her father, she cannot entertain the idea that she should give up her new life to look after him when he is old and ill. She uses the excuse that she is pregnant and the interests of the child should come first, but in reality she is selfish and protecting herself from helping Hobson. And yet, although she will not look after her father herself she sees the possibility that if Maggie and Will do so, the shop and its stock might eventually be left to them.

Like her sister Alice, Vickey remains a snob and is always ready to look down on Will because he is a mere bootmaker. She is indignant when Willie accuses her husband of being 'in trade' because she feels that her marriage to Fred Beenstock has taken her up the social ladder. Hobson sums up both his daughters at the end of the play when he says, 'They've got stiff necks with pride.'

In what ways is Vickey different from her sister Alice, and in what ways is she the same? Write your examples in lists and compare them.

We learn that Vickey is expecting a child. What do you think will be the main differences between this child's life and Vickey's own life with Hobson?

Do you think Vickey would be a pleasant or an unpleasant person to know? Give examples from the play to illustrate your opinion.

ALBERT PROSSER

Albert is Alice's young man and is of a slightly higher social class than the Hobsons, who are tradespeople while Albert is a solicitor. We first meet him when he comes into Hobson's shop to see Alice and is bullied by Maggie into buying a new pair of boots. He is very conscious of his own social position in the town and is very embarrassed at the thought of having 'to push a hand-cart through Salford in broad daylight!'

His aim in life is to make money and do well out of being a lawyer. He is, indeed, a competent lawyer and is able to stand up for himself against Hobson's rude remarks about the profession: 'Honest men live by business and lawyers live by laws.'

Albert is a self-confident young man, but is no match for Maggie and her organizing ways. He likes the sound of his own voice and has to be restrained from making a speech at Maggie and Will's wedding celebration. This time it is Alice who organizes him.

He is quick and observant, noticing the expensive hot-house flowers at the wedding and asking where Maggie and Will found the money to set up in business. Both he and Alice are concerned with their own material gain and are obviously well matched. Maggie sums him up when she says, 'Eh, Albert Prosser, I can see you're going to get on in the world.'

Why, do you think, should Albert want to marry Alice? What is it about her that attracts him?

Do you think Albert will make a good husband or not? Find some evidence from the play to support your opinion.

FRED BEENSTOCK

Fred plays a minor part in the play, portraying an ordinary young man, the son of a neighbouring tradesman who is quite suitable to marry Vickey. He is quite tactful when he comes with the news that Hobson was so drunk that he fell down the Beenstocks' cellar trap by phrasing it in a more kindly way; 'your father – wasn't looking very carefully where he was going and he fell into it.'

When Maggie and Will are married, Freddy is not very keen on lending a hand with the washing-up, saying 'Me wash pots!' He and Albert laugh at Willie's embarrassment at being left alone with Maggie on their wedding-night. 'He's afraid to be alone with her. That's what it is. He's shy of his wife.'

He is not a very strong character himself, allowing himself to be organized by Maggie, even though it is in his own interest. The young people, led by Maggie, blackmail Hobson into parting with money to enable Vickey and Alice to marry. Fred agrees to 'settle this matter out of court', the matter being Hobson's fall into the Beenstock cellar.

Imagine you are Fred Beenstock. Write out the conversation, in the form of a play, in which you, Albert and Maggie plan this trick on Henry Hobson.

MRS HEPWORTH

We meet Mrs Hepworth at the beginning of the play, when she comes into Hobson's shop and although she does not appear on stage again, she is very important because it is she who lends the money to Maggie and Willie to set up in business on their own. Without Mrs Hepworth's money they could not have become independent of Hobson.

We are told that she is of a higher social class than the Hobsons and the usual customers because she arrives in a carriage. She is patronizing and domineering, but values people if they are worth valuing which is why she praises Willie's excellent workmanship and why she later lends him money. She is clever enough to recognize a good investment.

Her speech is very straightforward; she does not mince words. She immediately tells Hobson to get up, 'You look ridiculous on the floor', and later says to him, 'hold your tongue'. She judges Hobson correctly when, after she has praised Willie's excellent workmanship, she says 'The man's a treasure, and I expect you underpay him.'

She obviously regards herself as a very important lady and behaves accordingly. How would you have felt if you had been one of the Hobson family in the shop when Mrs Hepworth comes into the shop? What differences do you think there would be between the reactions of Maggie and of Henry Hobson? Write two lists of feelings, one for Maggie and one for Henry, and compare them.

TIMOTHY WADLOW – 'TUBBY'

Tubby is the foreman bootmaker at Hobson's shop and he is described in the stage directions as 'A white-haired little man with thin legs and a paunch, in dingy clothes with no collar and a coloured cotton shirt. He has no coat on.'

Although he is the foreman, making boots is all he is good at and when he gets no orders from the shop he is lost. He refuses to take responsibility for making decisions after Maggie leaves Hobson's shop, saying, 'When you've told me what to do, I'll use my intelligence and see it's done properly.' However, Tubby must be very good at his job of bootmaking because it was he who had taught Willie, who becomes such a success.

After all the girls have left home to be married, Tubby remains loyal to Hobson. 'I'm an old servant of the master's, and I'm sticking to him now when everybody's calling me a doting fool because I don't look after Tubby Wadlow first.' However, he does feel that cooking Hobson's breakfast and waiting on him is no 'work for a foreman shoe hand'. In spite of this, he is still fair to others and a good judge of character, summing up Willie, Hobson and Maggie.

How would you have felt if you had been Tubby and had to lay tables and cook bacon for Hobson? Would you have thought it was fair?

Write a list of five words or phrases which you think describe Tubby's character.

JIM HEELER

Jim is a grocer and a friend of Hobson's who drinks with him at the 'Moonraker's'. Hobson needs someone to whom to tell all his troubles, especially his troubles with his daughters. Jim not only listens but flatters Hobson's powers of speaking, saying, 'You're an orator, Henry. I doubt John Bright himself is better gifted of the gab than you,' although he has to modify this praise with, 'Well, you're the best debater in the "Moonraker's" parlour.'

He has more common sense than Hobson, pointing out that in order to marry his girls off Hobson may have to provide marriage settlements, especially if the husbands are to be 'temperance'!

In Act IV when Tubby is cooking bacon for Hobson's breakfast and he bemoans the fact that the shop is losing money, Jim knows that Tubby is speaking out of turn even though he says, 'I'm telling no secret when I say it.' Jim believes, 'I don't think you ought to discuss that with me, Tubby.' We feel he is an honest man and a good friend to Hobson.

He has the same gift of the gab that he thinks Hobson has, using phrases such as, 'Roaring is mainly hollow sound,' and, 'it's steel in a man's character that subdues the woman'. He understands Hobson's weakness but is still his friend, standing up for him in the last act against Dr MacFarlane.

How do you think Hobson feels about Jim? Do you think Hobson is more fond of him than he is of his own daughters?

Jim seems very knowledgeable about women and marriage. What do you imagine his own family to be like?

ADA FIGGINS

Ada comes into the play to bring Willie's dinner in the scene in which Maggie has told him that they are to be married; the following conversation is no more than a squabble over Will which Maggie wins. Ada loses because she is no match for Maggie; in fact she is the complete opposite. She is described by the playwright as a 'weak, poor-blooded, poor-spirited girl of twenty, in clogs and shawl'. (page 18) She is honest and open, praising Will's ability to play the Jew's harp and says simply, 'I see the lad I love, Miss 'Obson.' The stage directions describe her as acting 'stupidly' and 'weakly', and she soon gives up her hold on Willie, saying, 'It's daylight robbery'.

It soon becomes clear that although Will is engaged to Ada, the match has been arranged by her mother, who 'had above a bit to do with it'. Willie tries to protest to Maggie about Ada's mother, saying, 'She's a terrible rough side to her tongue, has Mrs Figgins,' and when he realizes that he need never go back to his lodgings there again he thinks 'It's like an 'appy dream'.

Although Ada has been treated badly by Maggie and has been cheated of her young man, the audience does not feel especially sorry for her because there has not been enough time to get to know her and sympathize and also because we feel that Maggie has saved Willie from the dragon-like Mrs Figgins. Ada's purpose in the play is to serve as a minor block to Maggie's intention, which is soon overcome. It is quite amusing on stage to see such a trio, with Maggie quite easily dominating the other two and defeating Ada.

Imagine you are Ada. Write a short scene in which you tell your mother that you have lost Will.

DR MacFARLANE

The stage direction tells the actor playing the doctor that he has to be 'domineering' as indeed he needs to be if he is to get Henry Hobson to do as he is told. He is at first annoyed to be called out to see a

Characters: Dr MacFarlane

patient who is not even ill enough to be in bed, especially when he, the doctor, has been up all night delivering a baby. He will not tolerate the interference of Hobson's friend, Jim Heeler, and soon orders him to leave.

The scene soon becomes a battle of wills between the two men. Hobson sees it as a battle, saying, 'I've got to teach him a lesson. Scotchmen can't come over Salford lads this road'. The battle is particularly important since he regards Dr MacFarlane as 'a foreigner'. In fact it is the doctor who wins, treating Hobson's rudeness as an illness. 'Mr Hobson, if you don't mend your manners, I'll certify you for a lunatic asylum.'

When Hobson realizes that he cannot win against Dr MacFarlane he tries to pay him in order to get rid of him quickly. But the doctor, having diagnosed Hobson's illness as chronic alcoholism, knows that he can save him from dying and with Maggie's timely entrance has found the means to do it.

Dr MacFarlane has judged Hobson correctly and is more than equal to him in plain-speaking and bluntness. Hobson has to give in.

Write down your impression of Dr MacFarlane. Would you like him to treat you if you were ill? Give your reasons.

How do you think Hobson felt about the way the doctor spoke to him? Do you think Hobson deserved it?

Themes

(a) PRIDE COMES BEFORE A FALL

The main theme is the humiliating downfall of Henry Hobson. Its message is a warning about behaving in a pompous and arrogant way which will eventually lead to disgrace. However, it is not a tragedy. We are quite amused by the fall of Hobson because Maggie is an attractive person and we are pleased by her success.

Henry Hobson brings about his own fate. At the beginning of the play we see his high-handed attitude towards his three daughters and we realize that this cannot go on. Two of the daughters, Alice and Vickey, reject their father in their petty, snobbish way and it is left to Maggie and Will to look after him and support him.

Traditionally, an audience would enjoy seeing a pompous man made to look foolish on the stage. It is clear that his daughters know and understand him. Maggie says, 'I expect Mr Heeler's waiting for you in "Moonraker's", father,' after he had tried to give the impression that he was not going there. We soon gather that Hobson is no match for his daughter, Maggie, when she is determined on a course of action. It is the stubbornness of Hobson, his refusal to admit the truth about his own shop doing so badly, which makes his downfall take so long. He has set himself up as an important, prosperous man and it is very difficult for him to have to admit eventually that he needs Maggie and Will. Without them he would die of alcoholism and his shoemaking business would go bankrupt.

Harold Brighouse builds up Hobson's pride in himself although we, the audience, can see that Hobson cannot survive. At the end of the play we may feel sorry that Hobson has been humiliated but this is balanced by our pleasure that Maggie and Will are successful and will obviously continue to be so.

Activities

1. Imagine that you are Maggie or Will ten years after the end of the play and are explaining to your children how their grandfather comes to be living with them. How would you explain the fact that the two family businesses became combined? Remember that you have to be truthful but you cannot be unkind because your children's grandfather is still part of your family.

2. Write one or two paragraphs as if you were the publican, Sam Minns, defending Hobson against the way he is treated by Maggie and Will. Your listeners are likely to be the other 'regulars' at 'The Moonraker's'.

3. What is your opinion about the fate of Hobson? Do you think he deserved it or do you think the play should have ended differently?

You could write your views out as an argument or discussion between two members of the audience who have just seen the play.

(b) HARD WORK LEADS TO PROSPERITY

Another major theme of *Hobson's Choice* is a traditional one, that of the progress from rags to riches through solid, hard work. It would be familiar to the audience of 1916 from other plays, novels and poetry and would have been part of the moral upbringing of any Victorian family, reinforced by Church sermons and school.

Although Hobson himself is a self-made man who says, 'I'm a decent-minded man. I'm Hobson. I'm British middle class and proud of it', the playwright immediately lets us know that we should not approve of Hobson. The flaw in his character is one well known in Victorian popular literature – he drinks! At his first entrance he tries to pretend that he is merely going out for a few minutes, and is full of self-righteous indignation when his daughters reveal that they know he is going to the public house, 'The Moonraker's'. The only friends we hear about are drinking companions and Sam Minns, the publican, whose opinion Hobson respects concerning the fashions worn by his daughters. Although Hobson has in the past worked hard and has prospered, clearly now he leaves his shop to his daughters and spends his money and time drinking.

Compare Hobson with Willie Mossop. Will is an excellent craftsman, is shy and retiring and seems to lead an exemplary life. His talent combined with Maggie's determination to succeed is clearly going to outshine Hobson's achievement. His rise in fortune coincides with Hobson's decline simply because he works hard and Hobson does not. Hobson is resting on his laurels and is content to let other people work hard for him. Deprived of his two hardest workers, Maggie and Will, his shoemaking business soon declines.

The time-scale of the play is a mere thirteen months but in that time, through sheer hard work, Maggie and Will have ousted Hobson's shop and workshop as the main suppliers in the town. The moral is clear: Work hard and you will prosper.

Activities

1. How realistic do you find the rise in fortune of Maggie and Will? Should the playwright have made the time-gap longer? Argue your case as if it were 1916 and you could actually influence Mr Brighouse.

2. Maggie and Will borrowed money from Mrs Hepworth to start their business. Write the scene in which they persuade her to do this, setting out clearly how they hope to pay her back.

3. Write an alternative ending to the play in which Henry Hobson does not unite his company with that of Maggie and Will. Would the play still be a comedy?

(c) WOMEN'S INDEPENDENCE

The independence of women was a theme explored in plays from the 1880s onward and since this play, although set in the 1880s, was first performed during the First World War, the audience would be familiar with the idea that a woman could be practical and capable, and would be able to choose how to live her own life.

Although Maggie does not quite have the independence of spirit of some of Shaw's heroines, who choose not to marry, she does make her own choice of Will in spite of the opposition of her family. This opposition is shown to be merely snobbery. Even after Maggie and Will have been married for a year and have prospered, Alice still speaks contemptuously to her sister. 'Ah, well, a fashionable solicitor's wife doesn't rise so early as the wife of a working cobbler.'

Maggie's independence is contrasted with the lives of her two sisters who see themselves as their husband's wives rather than as independent women. It is true that at this time women were in general dependent upon men financially and did not yet have the right to vote for MPs in Parliament. Brighouse's audience would be familiar with the campaign that was launched before the First World War to obtain votes for women.

Maggie cannot be absolutely independent because she has no money, and since the acquisition of money underpins the morality of this play and is the attribute by which most of the characters are judged, she has to gain her independence by using Will. Although Brighouse allows a touch of affection, and, by the end of the play, mutual trust and respect between Will and Maggie, the bald truth is that Will is the only available vehicle for Maggie's ambition. She *has* to use him or be left an embittered old spinster waiting on her father.

Activities

1. Maggie is thirty when the play takes place. Why do you think she left it so long to set all these events in motion? You could write her reasons in the form of a diary.

2. Imagine that you are a friend of Will Mossop's. What arguments would you use to persuade him not to marry Maggie?

3. Maggie uses marriage to gain independence from her father. Make a list of any other ways she might have broken away from home in the 1880s. You will need to do some historical research.

(d) KINDS OF MARRIAGES

Of the three marriages in the play, Maggie and Will's is shown to be the least romantic. It is Maggie who pursues Willie, who has already been pursued and, apparently, captured by Ada Figgins and her mother. The conventional situation of two men fighting over a woman is reversed completely here with Will desperately protesting, 'Aren't you going to put up a better fight for me than that, Ada? You're fair giving me to her.'

The audience finds Will's timorous behaviour amusing in contrast to Maggie's determined ways. This shyness, combined with the natural polite good manners of employee to employer, leads him to plead, 'I'd really rather wed Ada, Maggie, if it's all same to you.'

The usual pattern of courtship, too, is reversed when Maggie proposes to Will in a most unromantic way. He is relieved when he thinks at first that it is a business partnership which Maggie is proposing and even when she makes clear that she intends marriage, he refers to the idea as a 'blow'. His first thought, that Maggie is proposing a business partnership, is, of course, the reason behind the marriage. She can see his business potential as a high-quality craftsman who, at the moment, lacks any drive or acumen, which she knows she can supply.

Themes: Kinds of marriages

The apparent contrast between Maggie's choice of Will and her sisters' choices is one of social class; but in fact all three marriages are based on the importance of money. It is money which decides social class in this play and although Alice's beau, Albert Prosser, and Vickey's choice, Freddy Beenstock, are middle-class, and Will at the beginning of the play is clearly working-class, by the end of the play, through a combination of hard work and marriage to the master's daughter, Will is their equal in prosperity and prospects.

However, Brighouse does not paint Maggie and Will's marriage as a business partnership only. Maggie insists, 'I want your hand in mine and your word for it that you'll go through life with me for the best we can get out of it,' and then softens it with, 'I've got the love all right.' Their marriage night is amusing with Will, after tentative thoughts of going into the bedroom, settling down to sleep on the sofa. Maggie 'takes him by the ear, and returns with him to bedroom' and so the audience is left at the end of Act III with the belief that Maggie is to be the dominant partner in this marriage – only to be disillusioned in Act IV. A year later the relationship is much more one of equals, with Will growing in confidence and now playing the role which Maggie has devised for him. However the marriage came into being it is clearly strong and amicable now, with Maggie and Will ending the play with the affectionate interchange, 'Eh, lad!' and 'Eh, lass!'

Activities

1. Imagine the scene when Ada Figgins arrives home with the news that she has lost Will to Maggie. Write a scene with the two characters, Ada and her mother, trying to show their feelings and plans.

2. What is your opinion about the way Maggie proposes to Will? Do you think it is a reasonable thing to do?

3. Which of the three marriages in the play do you think will be the most successful in ten years' time? You are a gossiping neighbour of

the Hobsons'. Write a letter to a friend discussing the marriages of the three girls.

(e) REGIONAL BACKGROUND

This play has a very distinct regional setting and is quite unlike, for example, Oscar Wilde's witty plays which were set in London about Londoners and played to London audiences. *Hobson's Choice* uses Lancashire dialect to some extent but more particularly the dialogue is characterized as plain, blunt speech. Brighouse also calls upon down-to-earth proverbial sayings such as, 'Courting's like that, my lass. All glitter and no use to nobody.'

The dialect is not so widely used nor so obscure that the play would not be understood outside the particular area in which it is set, but the dialogue is such that it demands to be spoken with a Salford accent.

Yet in spite of the play being so firmly set in the Victorian period and even more firmly set geographically, its relationships and themes have a universality which has meant that *Hobson's Choice* has been enacted many, many times since 1916. It is still a popular favourite with school and amateur dramatic groups, especially because of its two-fold attraction — realism and universality. Hobson's nineteenth-century, small-town values are mirrors of men's minds all over the world and in this lies the success of the play.

Activities

1. Imagine that you are a theatre critic for a London daily newspaper in 1916 and that you have just been to the first night on 22 June at the Apollo Theatre, London. Your job is to write a review giving your opinion of the play, remembering that you are reviewing a Lancashire comedy for a London audience.

Themes: **Regional background** 65

2. Do you think it would be possible to stage a successful version of *Hobson's Choice* if the actors could not speak with Lancashire accents? What, if anything, would be lost?

3. Imagine that you are the director of such a production. What advice would you give to your cast?

Questions on Hobson's Choice

You could try various ways of answering these questions: either in a single paragraph or in a full essay of about 800 to 1000 words. A simple rule to remember about an essay or examination answer is that it must have at least three paragraphs – a beginning, a middle and an end. As you become more practised at writing essays you will learn to plan your essays, perhaps as a list of points, then to sort them out into the order which seems best for your opinion and then to write the essay, expanding each of the points on your list into paragraphs. Remember that for every point you make, every opinion you have, you must have evidence from the play.

1. 'Will Mossop hasn't the spirit of a louse', says Vickey in Act IV of *Hobson's Choice*. How would you answer this criticism of Will? Would you agree or disagree?

2. At the end of the play, the author describes Hobson as looking 'pathetically' at Maggie and Will and then doing what he is told 'obediently'. Do you like this change in Hobson or do you prefer him as he was at the beginning of the play?

3. If you knew nothing else of the way young women behaved and were treated at the end of the nineteenth century, what impression would you be left with after meeting Maggie, Vickey and Alice Hobson and Ada Figgins in this play?

4. What is Hobson's attitude towards the women in his family in Act I? Has it changed radically by the end of the play?

5. Can you see any similarities in character between Maggie and her father? Are these similarities strengths or weaknesses?

6. Are you convinced by Willie's change of character between Act I and the end of Act IV? Do you think he will go on changing in the future or is his strength at the end of the play the end of his development?

7. *Hobson's Choice* is dominated by the Hobson family and yet there are several other minor characters who are interesting and important. If you could act one of these characters on stage yourself, who would you choose and why?

8. Maggie is a great organizer of other people's lives. If you were one of the other characters, what would have been your feelings about having your life organized by Maggie?

9. If you were directing this play and the actor playing Willie was unsure about how to behave onstage, what advice would you give him? You could give general advice about the whole play or take a short scene in much more detail.

10. Which of the characters in this play do you like best and which do you like least? Give several examples to support your opinion.

CONTEXT QUESTIONS

In some examinations you are allowed to take the copy of the book you are studying into the examination room as long as there are no notes in it and you have only the text in front of you. You are asked to read again quickly a portion of the book to refresh your memory and to write an examination answer with evidence from that context. Sometimes you are also asked to link themes or ideas in this short extract with the rest of the novel or play. The point of a question such as this is to make you concentrate on a small extract and write about that in detail.

As with a general essay, the answer to a context question also needs to be planned carefully so that you do not repeat yourself or omit an important point. Again, a list of points jotted down as they occur to you, rearranged and then expanded into at least a sentence and perhaps into a paragraph, will probably be the quickest way of organizing your answer.

1. Read again the beginning of the play until just before Hobson's entry, ending with Maggie saying, 'Courting's like that, my lass. All glitter and no use to nobody.'

What impression do you get from this extract of the characters of the three Hobson daughters?

2. Look again at Hobson's grumbling at his daughters from the bottom of page 4, 'Listen to me, you three. I've come to conclusions about you', as far as the top of page 8, 'So long as that's clear I'll go.'

If you were in the audience, what would your feelings be towards Hobson during this scene? Would you like him? Would you support him or his daughters? Do you think he is reasonable or unreasonable?

3. Mrs Hepworth's visit lasts from near the top of page 8, 'Good morning, Mrs Hepworth. What a lovely day!' to the top of page 11, 'Thinks she owns the earth because she lives at Hope Hall.'

Imagine you are Mrs Hepworth. Give your own version of this short scene as if you were telling one of your daughters at home. Why, later on in the play, do you lend Maggie and Will the money to start their own business?

4. Read again the scene in which Maggie proposes to Will, from halfway down page 14, 'Come up, and put the trap down; I want to talk to you,' to halfway down page 18, 'Ada would tell another story, though.'

Do you get the impression that this is a spur-of-the-moment action on Maggie's part or do you think she has been planning this proposal for some time? Give your reasons.

Do you think she is fair on Will or does she take advantage of her superior position?

5. Remind yourself fairly quickly of the scene in which Maggie and Will come back to the shop on their wedding-day, from the top of

page 30, 'I don't know what you're aiming at, Maggie, but –' to the bottom of page 33, 'Go on.'

What thoughts do you think are running through Will's mind in this scene? Is he pleased or embarrassed at being kissed by the girls? Do the girls believe he will ever take his 'proper place in this family' or will they always treat him badly?

6. Read again the scene in which the three young men are together, washing up after the wedding-feast, from halfway down page 41, 'Willie, we'll need this table when they're gone', to two-thirds of the way down page 43, 'Hurry up with those cups, Fred.'

In what ways is Will different from the other two young men? What is their attitude towards Will, do you think? Do you find Albert and Freddy likeable or not?

7. After Hobson wakes up in Beenstock's corn-cellar he comes straight round to Maggie for help. Read again from near the bottom of page 46, 'Now tell me what it is you came about?' to the top of page 51, 'You can settle with him here.'

What is it about the scandal that most upsets Hobson? Can you write an account of Hobson's fall into the corn-cellar as if you were reporting on the court case for the local paper? What aspects would you think were most important?

8. Read again Dr MacFarlane's visit to Hobson from page 64, 'Here's Doctor MacFarlane', to his exit.

Imagine you are the doctor and you have to write Hobson's medical notes when you get home, describing the nature of Hobson's illness and your attempts to help him to a cure. Write the notes in the form of a letter to another doctor indicating as well what your hopes are for Hobson's future.

9. Vickey and Alice arrive to see how their father is, after receiving Tubby Wadlow's messages. Read again the scene in which they excuse themselves from having to look after Hobson, from half-way down page 71, 'And I'm not your only daughter', to the bottom of page 77, 'Open the door for them, Will.'

Do you think the three girls have changed at all from the impression you had of them in Act I? Are Vickey and Alice exactly alike or are there clear differences in their characters?

Do you feel that Hobson knows his daughters well from the evidence in this extract?

10. Look again at the end of the play from the top of page 79, 'I've made him a proposal', to the end of the act.

Whose side are you on in the argument about the future of Hobson's business? Why? Do you think Maggie and Will drive too hard a bargain or do you think they are fair to Hobson? Would you have acted in the same way as Maggie and Will in their position?

Glossary

a come-by-chance: an illegitimate child born in the workhouse
a crack: a talk
a cut line: little profit in it
a foreigner: in this case, a Scot
afront: before
antimacassars: linen cloths to protect the backs of chairs from men's hair-oil
at owt: at anything else
axing: dialect for 'asking'

blood: well-dressed young man
boot shop: as becomes clear later, the shop sells boots, shoes and clogs, which are made in the cellar below
brass: money
brutalized childhood: has lived in poverty and may have been beaten
bumptious: over-confident

carriage folk: the people who can afford to keep carriages rather than walk
cedars of Lebanon: a Biblical reference
clogs: heavy, serviceable shoes

dunderheaded: stupid

efface: make himself invisible

fell on rest: a euphemism for 'has died'
finicking: fussy
Flat Iron market: a market with secondhand furniture

gaffer: boss
get my hand down: dig deep into my pockets
gifted of the gab: can use words eloquently
gradely: great deal

hash: mess
Hobson's Choice: this means there is no choice: only one course of action is open. The old saying comes from Thomas Hobson (*c*. 1544–1631) at whose stable the customers had no choice of horse but had to hire the next available one
hump added to nature: a bustle was pleated material at the

back of the dress, often padded

I ken: I know
I shouldn't marvel: I shouldn't be surprised

Jew's harp: a musical instrument
John Bright: a famous nineteenth-century political orator

libel: defamation of character by the spoken word
lief: willingly
Lord Beaconsfield: Benjamin Disraeli, Prime Minister

ma mannie: my man
Manchester Guardian: now called the *Guardian*, the most important national paper in that area
masonic emblems: marks and badges of Freemasons
Masons' meetings: Freemasonry: a group of men meeting together for mutual help and brotherly feeling
mill girls: traditionally dressed in clogs, skirts, blouses and shawls made, of course, out of cheap material
moithered: a version of mithered, which means 'troubled'

nobbut: nothing else but
nowt: nothing

nowty: uncertain

Old Harry: be very angry

parlour: the best sitting-room
Prince Consort: Prince Albert, husband to Queen Victoria

sagacity: wisdom
Salford: a former centre of the cotton-making industry near to Manchester
settlements: dowries, money given on marriage
shape: do anything
sheep's eyes: flirting, ogling
sixes and sevens: in a muddle
slackish: slovenly, untidy
slate: children in school used slate and chalk. It was cheaper than using paper because the slate could be wiped clean and re-used
summat: something

temperance young men: non-drinkers
the milk's spilt and I'll not cry: using the saying 'It's no use crying over spilt milk', meaning there is nothing to be done
the Queen: Queen Victoria
thraldom: spell
tokened: engaged
toper: an alcoholic
treading on my foot: getting in my way

uppishness: arrogance

victual you: feed you
visiting card: usually the name and address of the presenter. Often used as an introduction

Well, by gum: an alternative for the blasphemy, By God
What dost: What do you?
windbag: a man who says much but means little

worked up: they have so many boots unsold that they have used up all the available leather
workhouse brat: an illegitimate child, born in the workhouse
wrought up to point: ready to go through with it

yon: that place
you'll none rule me: you'll *not* rule me

MORE ABOUT PENGUINS, PELICANS, PEREGRINES AND PUFFINS

For further information about books available from Penguins please write to Dept EP, Penguin Books Ltd, Harmondsworth, Middlesex UB7 ODA.

In the U.S.A.: For a complete list of books available from Penguins in the United States write to Dept DG, Penguin Books, 299 Murray Hill Parkway, East Rutherford, New Jersey 07073.

In Canada: For a complete list of books available from Penguins in Canada write to Penguin Books Canada Limited, 2801 John Street, Markham, Ontario L3R 1B4.

In Australia: For a complete list of books available from Penguins in Australia write to the Marketing Department, Penguin Books Australia Ltd, P.O. Box 257, Ringwood, Victoria 3134.

In New Zealand: For a complete list of books available from Penguins in New Zealand write to the Marketing Department, Penguin Books (N.Z.) Ltd, Private Bag, Takapuna, Auckland 9.

In India: For a complete list of books available from Penguins in India write to Penguin Overseas Ltd, 706 Eros Apartments, 56 Nehru Place, New Delhi 110019.

PENGUIN BOOKS OF POETRY

- *American Verse*
- *Ballads*
- *British Poetry Since 1945*
- *A Choice of Comic and Curious Verse*
- *Contemporary American Poetry*
- *Contemporary British Poetry*
- *Eighteenth-Century Verse*
- *Elizabethan Verse*
- *English Poetry 1918–60*
- *English Romantic Verse*
- *English Verse*
- *First World War Poetry*
- *Georgian Poetry*
- *Irish Verse*
- *Light Verse*
- *London in Verse*
- *Love Poetry*
- *The Metaphysical Poets*
- *Modern African Poetry*
- *New Poetry*
- *Poems of Science*
- *Poetry of the Thirties*
- *Post-War Russian Poetry*
- *Spanish Civil War Verse*
- *Unrespectable Verse*
- *Victorian Verse*
- *Women Poets*

PLAYS IN PENGUINS

- ☐ Edward Albee *Who's Afraid of Virginia Woolf?*
- ☐ Alan Ayckbourn *The Norman Conquests*
- ☐ Bertolt Brecht *Parables for the Theatre (The Good Woman of Setzuan/The Caucasian Chalk Circle)*
- ☐ Anton Chekhov *Plays (The Cherry Orchard/The Three Sisters/Ivanov/The Seagull/Uncle Vania)*
- ☐ Henrik Ibsen *Hedda Gabler/Pillars of Society/The Wild Duck*
- ☐ Eugène Ionesco *Absurd Drama (The Rhinoceros/The Chair/The Lesson)*
- ☐ Ben Jonson *Three Comedies (Volpone/The Alchemist/Bartholomew Fair)*
- ☐ D. H. Lawrence *Three Plays (The Collier's Friday Night/The Daughter-in-Law/The Widowing of Mrs Holroyd)*
- ☐ Arthur Miller *Death of a Salesman*
- ☐ John Mortimer *A Voyage Round My Father/What Shall We Tell Caroline?/The Dock Brief*
- ☐ J. B. Priestley *Time and the Conways/I Have Been Here Before/The Inspector Calls/The Linden Tree*
- ☐ Peter Shaffer *Amadeus*
- ☐ Bernard Shaw *Plays Pleasant (Arms and the Man/Candida/The Man of Destiny/You Never Can Tell)*
- ☐ Sophocles *Three Theban Plays (Oedipus the King/Antigone/Oedipus at Colonus)*
- ☐ Arnold Wesker *The Wesker Trilogy (Chicken Soup with Barley/Roots/I'm Talking about Jerusalem)*
- ☐ Oscar Wilde *Plays (Lady Windermere's Fan/A Woman of No Importance/An Ideal Husband/The Importance of Being Earnest/Salomé)*
- ☐ Thornton Wilder *Our Town/The Skin of Our Teeth/The Matchmaker*
- ☐ Tennessee Williams *Sweet Bird of Youth/A Streetcar Named Desire/The Glass Menagerie*

ENGLISH AND AMERICAN LITERATURE IN PENGUINS

☐ *Emma* Jane Austen

'I am going to take a heroine whom no one but myself will much like,' declared Jane Austen of Emma, her most spirited and controversial heroine in a comedy of self-deceit and self-discovery.

☐ *Tender is the Night* F. Scott Fitzgerald

Fitzgerald worked on seventeen different versions of this novel, and its obsessions – idealism, beauty, dissipation, alcohol and insanity – were those that consumed his own marriage and his life.

☐ *The Life of Johnson* James Boswell

Full of gusto, imagination, conversation and wit, Boswell's immortal portrait of Johnson is as near a novel as a true biography can be, and still regarded by many as the finest 'life' ever written. This shortened version is based on the 1799 edition.

☐ *A House and its Head* Ivy Compton-Burnett

In a novel 'as trim and tidy as a hand-grenade' (as Pamela Hansford Johnson put it), Ivy Compton-Burnett penetrates the facade of a conventional, upper-class Victorian family to uncover a chasm of violent emotions – jealousy, pain, frustration and sexual passion.

☐ *The Trumpet Major* Thomas Hardy

Although a vein of unhappy unrequited love runs through this novel, Hardy also draws on his warmest sense of humour to portray Wessex village life at the time of the Napoleonic wars.

☐ *The Complete Poems of Hugh MacDiarmid*

☐ Volume One
☐ Volume Two

The definitive edition of work by the greatest Scottish poet since Robert Burns, edited by his son Michael Grieve, and W. R. Aitken.

ENGLISH AND AMERICAN LITERATURE IN PENGUINS

☐ **Main Street Sinclair Lewis**

The novel that added an immortal chapter to the literature of America's Mid-West, *Main Street* contains the comic essence of Main Streets everywhere.

☐ **The Compleat Angler Izaak Walton**

A celebration of the countryside, and the superiority of those in 1653, as now, who love *quietnesse, vertue* and, above all, *Angling*. 'No fish, however coarse, could wish for a doughtier champion than Izaak Walton' – Lord Home

☐ **The Portrait of a Lady Henry James**

'One of the two most brilliant novels in the language', according to F. R. Leavis, James's masterpiece tells the story of a young American heiress, prey to fortune-hunters but not without a will of her own.

☐ **Hangover Square Patrick Hamilton**

Part love story, part thriller, and set in the publands of London's Earls Court, this novel caught the conversational tone of a whole generation in the uneasy months before the Second World War.

☐ **The Rainbow D. H. Lawrence**

Written between *Sons and Lovers* and *Women in Love*, *The Rainbow* covers three generations of Brangwens, a yeoman family living on the borders of Nottinghamshire.

☐ **Vindication of the Rights of Woman Mary Wollstonecraft**

Although Walpole once called her 'a hyena in petticoats', Mary Wollstonecraft's vision was such that modern feminists continue to go back and debate the arguments so powerfully set down here.

Penguin Passnotes

This comprehensive series, designed to help O-level and CSE students, includes:

Subjects

Biology
Chemistry
Economics
English Language
French
Geography

Human Biology
Mathematics
Modern Mathematics
Modern World History
Narrative Poems
Physics

Literature

Arms and the Man
Cider With Rosie
Great Expectations
Jane Eyre
Kes
Lord of the Flies
A Man for All Seasons
The Mayor of Casterbridge
My Family and Other Animals
Pride and Prejudice

The Prologue to the
  Canterbury Tales
Pygmalion
Saint Joan
She Stoops to Conquer
Silas Marner
To Kill a Mockingbird
War of the Worlds
The Woman in White
Wuthering Heights

Shakespeare

As You Like It
Henry IV, Part I
Henry V
Julius Caesar
Macbeth
The Merchant of Venice
A Midsummer Night's Dream
Romeo and Juliet
Twelfth Night